TRUE FRIEND

Leyla Welkin Ph.D.

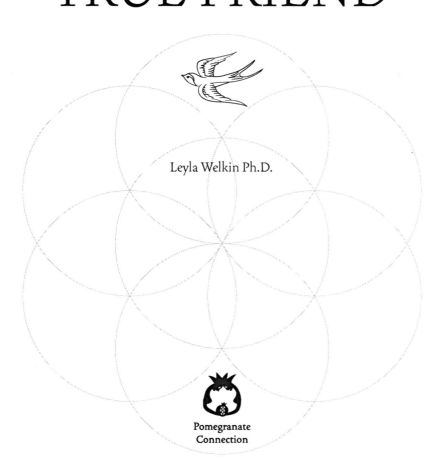

Pomegranate
Connection

TRUE FRIEND

FOR WOMEN
WHO HAVE EXPERIENCED SEXUAL ABUSE:

HOW TO BE A FRIEND TO YOURSELF
HOW TO BE A TRUE FRIEND TO A SURVIVOR

Leyla Welkin Ph.D.

Pomegranate
Connection

© 2014 Leyla Welkin
Graphic Design: Gülru Höyük
All Rights Reserved.

No part of this publication may be reproduced, stored in a retrieval system, or transmitted, in any form or by any means, electronic, mechanical, photocopying, recording, or otherwise, without the written permission of the author.

First published by Dog Ear Publishing
4010 W. 86th Street, Ste H
Indianapolis, IN 46268
www.dogearpublishing.net

ISBN: 978-0-6157-5111-5

This book is printed on acid free paper.

Printed in the United States of America

Author's note

Leyla Welkin is a clinical cross cultural psychologist who has practiced psychotherapy, taught as an intercultural educator and developed programs in those fields for thirty years. Her birth in Gaziantep, Turkey to American parents began a life lived between many cultural worlds. She received her interdisciplinary Master's and Doctoral degrees in the United States and worked for many years there in outpatient clinics and in private practice with women and families struggling with the effects of sexual and family abuse. She also began teaching in university psychology and counseling programs in 1995. In 2008 Leyla returned to Turkey and founded the Pomegranate Connection program in Ankara. She continues to provide research, training and consultation services internationally through the Pomegranate Connection and can be reached at welkin.l@gmx.com

Acknowledgements and Gratitude

This book is the fruit of thirty years of clinical practice and of four years of collaboration with the warm and generous Turkish colleagues and friends who contributed to the original Turkish edition. DOST, our original Turkish version, was truly a labor of love for all the people involved. We are proud to have produced two separate editions in Turkish. The first edition was fully distributed to women's NGOs, health care providers, shelter house workers, police, lawyers, psychologists, educators and social service workers within three months of its printing. Nearly half the copies of our second edition were ordered before that book was even printed. Clearly this common sense, easily accessible and strengths based guide filled a need.

In particular I want to thank some people without whom this book would never have been written. First and foremost I want to express my gratefulness to the many women, men and children who participated in women's sexual abuse survivors groups, family therapy sessions and individual and couple work with me. I salute their courage and insight. I want to acknowledge the honor given to me by their trust as we worked and learned together about how abusive relationships harm and healthy relationships heal. Their generous gift has been more important than any other contribution to the quality of this work.

I also want to acknowledge the tremendous contributions of many colleagues and friends who guided, supported and joined me on this journey. Leticia Nieto, Kathleen O'Shaunessy and Diana Eck were important teachers. Ron O'Connor, Pamela Newman and Sandia Slaby taught me more than I can say. Selçuk Candansayar and Aslıhan Sayin were wonderful partners and opened the door for me to working in Turkey. I cannot name all the wonderful women and men in Turkey who opened their hearts, their homes and their organizations to me and shouldered alongside me many of the tasks that were involved in developing this book. But a few people must be named. I apologize for the names I am leaving out, not because their aid is forgotten, but because the number of supporters and friends I found were literally countless. Everyone who volunteered for or helped in any way with the work of the Pomegranate Connection Program has my eternal gratitude: Sevinç Unal, Nuran Kızılkan, Ayşe Nur Yılmazer, Mervi Nousiainen, Merve Kan, Aylin Ülkümen, Fatma Akansel, Gülru Höyük, Aşiyan Suleymanoğlu, Rauf Kenan Arun, Selçuk Aslan, Kemal Arıkan and Ahmet Hayta were indispensible colleagues and friends. Emine Onaran İncirlioğlu, Çiğdem Atakuman, Mary Anne McFarlane, Berin Çanlı, and Jodie Das provided friendship and professional support that made the whole thing possible. I also want to give special thanks to the public and cultural affairs staff at the U.S. Embassy in Ankara: Todd Pierce, Craig Dicker, Ayşegül Taşkın, Nurdan Akbulut and Stefanie Altman-Winans. They recognized the value of my work early and gave me opportunities and support.

My own family has always been one of my most important resources and I want to thank my sons Evan and Avery Welkin, my sister Marcy Summers, my brothers, Ross Brown and Craig Jacobrown, and my parents, Jack and Judy Brown, for the adventurous, creative, fun loving and resourceful start they gave me in life and that they continue to encourage today.

May we all find the resources of kind and generous people that we need and may times of trouble pass quickly. I firmly believe that a better world is possible and that we are all engaged in the sacred process of building heaven here on earth. May we open our eyes and hearts to see it, may we discover the joy and beauty that lives all around us. "Thou hast given so much to me, give one thing more, a grateful heart."

TABLE OF CONTENTS

Introduction | *15*
    Consent, Power and Survivors | *17*
    What This Guide Does Not Cover | *19*
    Breaking the Silence | *21*

I. Being Your Own Best Friend | *23*
    Familiar Pain | *25*
    1. Know Yourself | *29*
    2. The Body-Mind System | *31*
        Kids at a Dance | *31*
        The Body-Mind System | *31*
            Three Level Brain Diagram | *31*
        When Abuse Occurs | *34*
    3. Immediate Emotional Effects | *39*
        Fear, Anger and Sadness | *39*
        Problems Regulating Emotions | *41*
            Sympathetic and Parasympathetic Nervous System Diagram | *41*
    4. Complicating Factors | *44*
        1. Age and Development | *44*
        2. Repeated Occurrence | *45*
        3. Relationship to the Abuser | *46*
        4. Finding Safety and Support | *47*
        5. Vulnerabilities Before the Abuse | *49*
        6. Perceived Severity of the Abuse | *50*

5. Complex Post Traumatic Stress Disorder | 53
    Chart from Herman | 53
    List of Behaviors | 55
6. Problems with Consciousness and Thoughts | 57
7. Problems with Relationships | 59
    Serious Problems with Trust | 59
    "Bad Radar" | 59
    Poor Self Image | 59
    Isolation and Withdrawal | 60
    Sexual Problems | 60

II. The Recovery Process: How Do We Heal? | 61
1. Finding Safety | 63
    Healing Stories | 64
    Body-Mind Healing | 66
    What is Internal Safety? | 66
        Autonomic Nervous System Diagram | 68
    Creating Internal Safety | 70
        TRY THIS
        Steps to Finding Safety | 70
        Full Body Breath | 72
        Automatic Thoughts | 74
        Noticing Thoughts | 75
2. Facing the Pain | 76
    Memory | 76
    Coping and Soothing Ourselves | 79
    Everything is Interpretation; Interpretation is Everything | 80
        TRY THIS
        Test Your Version of the Truth | 82
    Mindfulness and the Here and Now | 84

> *TRY THIS*
> Being in the Here and Now | *85*
> 5-4-3-2-1 Exercise | *86*

3. Building Support and Trust | *89*
   Blaming the Victim | *89*
   Choosing the Right Friends | *90*
   > *TRY THIS*
   > Choosing Your Friends Well | *92*
   > *"A True Friend Does Not" List* | *93*
   Staying in Charge of Your Own Healing | *94*

4. Making a New Story | *97*
   Interpreting Again | *97*
   > *TRY THIS*
   > Writing the Story Down | *99*
   > Facts/Values/Evaluations | *100*
   Reframing Destructive Thoughts | *104*

5. Moving On | *108*
   Recovery, Confidence, Empowerment | *108*
   Goal Setting and Recovery | *109*
   > *TRY THIS*
   > Where Will You Be When You Have Recovered? | *109*
   > What is the Road to Your New Life? | *111*
   > First Steps | *111*
   Expecting Miracles But Not Magic | *113*

III. Being A True Friend | *119*
1. Why True Friends Are So Important | *121*
   The Rescue Triangle | *123*
   > *Rescue Triangle Diagram* | *123*
2. Secondary Trauma | *130*
   Risks to the Survivor | *130*

Risks to the Helper | *133*

3. Boundaries - What Are They? | *136*

Know Your Limits | *136*

Keep Your Own Emotional Balance | *137*

Don't Let Someone Else's Crisis Become Yours | *139*

Pay Close Attention to Your Own Needs when Helping Others | *140*

TRY THIS

Keeping Healthy Boundaries - Saying "No" | *141*

4. For Partners and Family Members of Sexual Abuse Survivors | *144*

Sexuality Issues | *144*

Trust and Intimacy | *146*

Strength after Healing, Real Intimacy | *147*

5. What Services Does a Survivor Need? | *149*

Protect, Prosecute & Prevent | *149*

Recovery Map Diagram | *150*

Health Issues | *151*

Legal Issues | *151*

Basic Practical Needs, Social Services | *152*

Interviewing Survivors | *154*

Steps to Remember | *154*

TRY THIS

Body Scan | *156*

Rest, Relax and Rejuvenate: Guided Imagery | *159*

6. Strength After Healing Together | *162*

A Systemic Approach | *162*

An Ant's World System | *163*

An Ant's World System Diagram | *164*

7. Balancing a Human Rights Orientation with a Social Contract | *168*

Glossary | *171*

Resources & References | *173*

Dedicated in loving memory and joy to Leyla Sevinçli.

You are not alone as long as you stand with yourself and find your true friends.

INTRODUCTION

This book is a three part handbook for women who have experienced sexual exploitation or abuse. It was designed for any woman who has experienced sexual abuse, either immediately after a bad experience or when she is looking back on an experience in the past. The first section begins with a few typical stories of abuse experiences and then outlines how abuse tends to affect people who experience it. The second section of this guide describes some specific things that survivors can do to help themselves heal and some of the stages they can expect to go through in the process of healing. The third part of this guide is written for the people who want to help and be a true friend to a survivor. Family members, partners, husbands, friends and people who voluntarily or professionally want to support the healing of sexual abuse survivors will find practical guidance in this section. We finish with a short discussion of why the protection and healing of sexual abuse survivors, the prosecution of people who are abusive, and the prevention of sexual abuse benefits society as a whole.

All three sections of this guide are laid out describing a series of steps or areas of focus. But please do not imagine that there is a perfect sequence, a necessary path from point A to B to C for healing. Every person is different and every experience is different. Survivors of sexual abuse and exploitation have many things in common. But they also have aspects of their experiences that are individually unique to them. No two people were harmed in exactly the same way, nor will any two people heal in exactly the same way. Over many years of working with survivors in different parts of the world, we have learned a few things. This handbook is an attempt to offer simple, specific information that we hope will be useful for many survivors of sexual abuse and exploitation and their supporters.

One of the most painful aspects of sexual exploitation is that it often leaves a girl or woman feeling terribly alone. Most girls and women who have been mistreated sexually have the feeling that they have done something wrong and that they have been singled out as uniquely bad, dirty, or immoral. Too often they feel ashamed and isolated. This book seeks to break through the isolation and the shame that keeps women silent and alone after abuse. There are many books that discuss the difficulties of women who have been abused and ways to recover. This book is different because it focuses on the relational side of the abuse and the recovery process.

Unlike most of the self-help books and guides for working with sexual abuse survivors that are already available, this guide places relationships and the importance of human relatedness at the center of the healing process. The ability to build and maintain strong, healthy human relationships and families is the highest priority for many cultures and people in the world. This guide gives that value a central place. The individual human rights orientation of so much of the psychological and legal literature about abuse is important and valuable. But this individual focus has sometimes obscured the centrality of the relationships that sustain our lives. Balancing individual needs, rights and priorities with social and family relatedness, responsibility and accountability is fundamental to living a psychologically and biologically healthy life.

Consent, Power and Survivors

The shame and isolation brought about by abuse is based on falsehoods. No matter what may have led up to rape, molestation, or sexual harassment, the victim is never responsible for the exploitation. No matter what a person does, no matter how she behaves, she is not responsible for the behavior of someone who is older, stronger, more powerful, more socially prominent, or more knowledgeable than she is.

Sexual behaviors or actions are based upon decisions and choices. There is a fundamental difference between feeling desire, having a sexual impulse, and sexual behaviors acted out on others. Healthy adults are able to separate internal impulses from outward actions. It is not always easy, but making conscious choices about acting on impulses is a fundamental part of healthy human behavior. Even seductive behavior or actions interpreted as provocative do not amount to consent to another person's sexual acts. Any person who forces any kind of unwanted sexual act upon another person is responsible for their own behavior. Consent is fundamental to all healthy sexual behavior. Children cannot give consent; they do not have the necessary knowledge or understanding of consequences. People who are drunk, asleep, mentally disabled or in a position where withholding consent would threaten their well being, are not able to give the real consent that is required for healthy sex. Without full, conscious, non-coerced consent, sex acts become rape or molestation.

To feel sexual desire is completely natural, but desire is separate from behavior. Whether sexual behavior is coerced, forced, or chosen depends upon many factors, but the distinctions between these behaviors are all about power. Because power is an integral part of all human relationships, sexual behavior always occurs in the context of power. Relative levels of power between two people are complex and often not obvious. But we can make some firm statements. Some people are in a position to exercise greater power in relationships. Those who are physically stronger, or older, have more knowledge, or who have more mental capacity wield additional power. Moreover, if a person has higher social status, or has greater social rank, like an employer or a workplace superior, they have more social power.

Another important distinction is between influence and power. Parents for instance know that their children, though less powerful, are nonetheless very influential over their parents. But influence, without the social position or institutions to back it up, is not the same as the power wielded by parents or employers, husbands or people in authority. Interdependence is a reality; people with superior power depend upon the cooperation and agreement of their subordinates. But the difference between influence and power is that people with more power determine the rules of the game for everyone. There are privileges attached to dominant social positions. People with less power must work harder and do more to adapt to rules and circumstances that have been set up for the convenience and benefit of those with more power. Having influence is not the same as the ability to direct others and hold authority.

The sad truth is that the large majority of sexual abuse in the world happens when a person with more power takes advantage of their privilege to gain sexual satisfaction from a person who should be able to trust them. Abusers most often target a family member, a subordinate or someone who thinks of them as a friend. Sexual abuse and exploitation depend on the misuse of power and violations of trust. The sexual aspect of this exploitation is important because sexual abuse affects people at a deep, intimate level. But more than an expression of sexual desire, sexual abuse is a deep violation of trust through the misuse of interpersonal power.

Throughout this text we have used the term survivor instead of using the more common term victim. This is a conscious choice. We want to emphasize that after an experience of victimization, people who survive always have the opportunity to heal fully. The use of the term victim tends to become a limit and a burden. To be a victim defines us forever by a bad experience. Survivors have gone beyond that experience and have put it into their history. A survivor is no longer defined by something that happened in the past, she has overcome it.

Most survivors wish that somehow they could turn back the clock and return to a time before the abuse occurred. The fear and pain associated with a survivor's memories, shame and self-blame can be overwhelming. Many people wish they could feel better without ever having to face their pain or trust other people again. At the same time, many people are often terrified to face life so alone. This guide is written on the premise that no one should have to live without the healthy support and caring of others. Full healing requires facing challenges and learning to build healthy trust. The process of healing from sexual abuse and exploitation involves learning to have healthy, supportive relationships, building solidarity, and becoming more socially skillful. For some abuse survivors healing has a lot to do with regaining lost confidence. For some survivors, healing means learning self confidence for the first time.

What This Guide Does Not Cover

It is very common for survivors of abuse to waste lots of energy worrying about why the abuser acted the way he did, instead of using that energy to take care of herself. In fact, a survivor of abuse must focus first on her own healing, not on the abuser. This book does not go into detail about the social, psychological and biological problems that underlie or motivate people who are abusive. That is a separate and complex issue that cannot be covered in a short guide. The motivations, causes, excuses and problems of perpetrators of abuse are not the problem, nor the priority of a person who has been abused. In fact, only after a survivor has regained her own health and balance is she in a position to focus on mending her relationships with abusive people.

There are some additional things that this book does not address. Because there is evidence that worldwide, the large majority of sexual abuse is of girls and women by older, stronger, more socially powerful boys and men, this book is written first for those girls and women. We do not want to imply that sexual abuse of boys and men by other boys and men, or by older girls and women is not important or significant. However, there are special issues for boys and men after abuse that we will not discuss here.

This guide is also not designed to address many of the special issues for children and young girls. When working with children, a helper must have special knowledge about child development that we will not discuss in detail here. We have focused on a guide for adults who can help care for themselves and make decisions about their own lives.

In addition, abuse of other vulnerable people, for instance those with physical disabilities, or frail older people is not uncommon. People from social groups that suffer discrimination are also more easily exploited, for instance gay or transgendered people and ethnic or racial minorities. All these forms of abuse and exploitation are harmful, wrong and must be confronted and stopped.

We hope people from different vulnerable groups who have experienced sexual abuse will find useful information in this guide. Many points in the process of both harm and of healing will be familiar to any survivor. But rather than try to be comprehensive and meet the needs of all survivors, this book has been designed to address the most common types of abuse. We hope that more specific guides for people from special groups will follow. Boys, men, people with different gender or sexuality orientations, and people from socially disempowered groups should take what they can use from this handbook and leave the rest. In fact, we hope everyone will use the information they find helpful and set aside the things that do not seem to apply to them.

Breaking the Silence

There is no single way to heal from sexual abuse; there are many ways. But one thing is certain. If survivors of sexual abuse are going to find real healing, an important part of that healing will be in the new, stronger, more flexible, more reliable and more encouraging relationships that survivors learn to build. Those new, healthier relationships will be formed within the survivor, with other survivors, and with true friends and allies that can be found everywhere. There are people everywhere who care about and want to stand in solidarity with survivors of sexual abuse.

The authors of this guide are proud to be among the many allies of girls and women who have suffered from sexual abuse and exploitation. We expect that one of the most important contributions this handbook will make is to increase the likelihood of survivors speaking up about their abuse. Speaking up makes it possible to find safety and allies. It allows survivors to create friendships of solidarity and support.

Silence does not protect us; it is part of the wound. Our vision of a world without sexual abuse will have been realized when sexual abuse is no longer a source of shame and isolation but instead a matter for social concern. Humanity will have accomplished something very important when exploitation can be spoken about more easily, when abuse evokes immediate caring, and when society holds exploiters accountable. For this to happen, appropriate treatment must be available both for survivors and for those who have harmed them. Accountability for perpetrators of abuse, and education, treatment and support for both perpetrators and survivors, will be ordinary in a world that prevents sexual abuse. This handbook is a contribution toward that goal and that vision.

PART I

Being Your Own Best Friend

Familiar Pain:

Ayshe was six and loved to play hide and seek with the children in her neighborhood. The warm, spring air and sunshine had coaxed flowers into bloom and the children were full of bouncy excitement. Mehmet, Ayshe's 13 year old cousin, was a little old for some of the games, but it made the adults feel better to have an older boy playing with the younger children, watching over them. Jon was "it" and crooked his arm over his eyes. He counted to 50 as fast as he could push out the numbers, while the rest of the children scattered giggling, finding hiding places.

Ayshe found a fence and slipped around the corner behind it, not a great hiding place, but she was too excited to think much, and besides she wanted to watch Jon counting. Jon was a favorite of hers in the neighborhood, so funny and kind. She watched with one eye peeking around the corner of the fence as he counted. Mehmet ran up to her from behind, pulled her arm and whispered urgently,

"This is a bad spot! Here, let me show you a better one." He tugged, guiding her further away toward a dark doorway into an empty courtyard. Ayshe trusted his choice. He was much older than she was. He was her protector, meant to look after her. He was teaching her not to get caught. She followed willingly and when they got inside the dark doorway, she tried to peek around the corner again. But Mehmet pulled her back.

"No, don't, he will see you!" Mehmet tightened his grip on her arm and pulled her further into the courtyard... Ayshe followed him behind a metal oil tank and he pulled her around in front of him, embracing her from behind so that she felt cupped against his body.

At first she liked the feeling of being held firmly by the big boy. He seemed so smart and strong, they wouldn't be found here for a long time. But then something shifted and a flash of fear prickled up her spine. Mehmet's grasp on her had tightened. One of his hands slipped down between her legs and he pulled her closer against him. His fingers were moving around too much, she felt hot with alarm and began to struggle to pull away.

"No stay! Don't worry; I won't hurt you. We're hiding." Mehmet whispered urgently in her ear, tightening his hold while she pulled away. Ayshe was confused. What was he doing? Was he really trying to help her hide? What was this urgent and strange tone in his voice? But she stopped struggling and held her breath. He held her and his fingers kept moving. It took a long while before they finally stepped out of the hiding place and ran toward the base, yelling "I'm free!"

That was how it started. For the next few years Mehmet found Ayshe again and again when the neighborhood children played. Sometimes, when they were hiding during hide and seek, he showed her special hidden places. Sometimes he played other games with her that she didn't like. But Mehmet was older, bigger and he told her it was OK. He was her protector and the adults told her he was taking care of her. She thought maybe she was special; maybe she was his favorite. But after a while he said too many times that this was a secret between them. Then he began to turn away and make fun of her in front of the other kids. The time came when she began to feel as if the games were not fun at all. Something in her told her it was wrong. She felt ashamed.

By the time Ayshe was a teenager, she felt painfully uncomfortable about this secret and wished she could forget it. She had a feeling that these incidents would never have happened if she had done something different or had told her parents. But it was so embarrassing to think about telling anyone her ugly secret. She tried to pretend it hadn't happened. Maybe she didn't really remember it correctly. Maybe she was exaggerating the thing in her own imagination. But in the back of her mind, she felt as if she was a dirty person, someone who did bad things and might not be able to find a really good boyfriend. What if people found out about her? Wouldn't she be even more ashamed?

****

Natalie *was excited to be at university. At 18 she had never lived away from her parents before. But this opportunity to attend a good university in a larger city was a* *privilege she had earned by doing well on the national exam. She didn't want to pass up this chance. She lived in a girl's dormitory with many friends. The first year students in the department formed a number of friendship groups and most of the time she was with her girl friends. From time to time, a mixed group of young men and women would sit together eating snacks or drinking tea in the evening. She felt very grown up in these gatherings.*

She noticed Jordan early in the second semester. He was smart and seemed to have had a lot of experiences. He told stories of his adventures in his hometown with a group of schoolmates. She wasn't sure that all the things he described were true. But it didn't matter, he was fun to listen to, and the stories were exciting: jumping off of a bridge into river water deep below; riding too many boys on a bicycle and just avoiding injury in a terrible crash into a parked car. He described leaping off and rolling down the side of the road. Jordan was daring.

Natalie thought about Jordan, even when he wasn't around; and it seemed as if he had begun to notice her too. She was flattered when he told her he wanted to spend some time talking just with her. Even though her mother had always warned her not to be alone with a boy, she thought, what could happen? I will be fine. One day, after they had met a few times privately sitting and talking on the football pitch benches, he took her walking.

She was surprised when he took her to a vacant lot where an old house had been partly demolished. A few parts of the block walls still stood. They sat inside the ruin and he pulled out a pack of cigarettes, coaxing her to try one. She sucked on the lit cigarette he put between her lips. She coughed and laughed; feeling light headed and excited. When he took the cigarette out of her mouth and began to kiss her lips, she thought it felt lovely.

But the warm feeling in her belly turned to confusion when he pushed his hand down her top and forced her to lie back on the rubble. Wait a minute. This was more than she was ready for! But now it seemed too late to protest. He was pushing her down, and she was suddenly ashamed at having been persuaded into this private time in a dangerous place. Who would believe her if she said she didn't want sex? Jordan was telling her it would be OK. No one would ever have to know. This was just their secret. He would never tell. He loved her he said; didn't she love him? His words rushed around her mind, confusing her further.

Her mother's voice echoed in her mind behind his words. Good girls are never alone with young men. Time alone with men was for marriage only. A good, honorable girl knows how to tell a man no. An honorable girl would never allow herself to be talked into anything. Maybe she wasn't a good girl after all. Maybe she was a bad girl and that was how she had gotten herself into this mess. Natalie held still under Jordan and tried to slip away from the stony ruin in her mind; she tried not to feel anything.

1. Know Yourself

According to the World Health Organization "available data suggest that in some countries nearly one in four women may experience sexual violence by an intimate partner, and up to one-third of adolescent girls report their first sexual experience as forced." (WHO 149) In most of the world the stigma of sexual abuse is so great there are no reliable statistics. But we do know that these stories are descriptions of experiences that are far too common. Ayshe and Natalie's reactions, as described in these stories, are based on work with many survivors around the world and follow a pattern that is painfully familiar. Girls should be able to trust friends, relatives, teachers, and neighbors, people who are meant to protect and care for them. Sometimes a girl or woman puts her trust in the wrong person and she is violated. She expects to be treated with respect and kindness and instead the older, stronger, more experienced person takes advantage of her trust and pushes past her safety and comfort. Why do people do this? Very simply, the reason a person takes advantage of another's trust is to satisfy his own needs. Exploiters are not considering the girl's needs or desires. They are focused only on satisfying themselves.

We all live in societies that behave as if some people are more important, more valuable, more worthy of respect and benefits than others. We all learn very early that not everyone is given the same respect. Some people, for a variety of reasons, decide that their needs should be met, regardless of the costs or affects on others. Some people develop a sense of special entitlement; exploitation is a simple extension of that belief. Sexual abuse is just one form of exploitative behavior. Unfortunately, virtually all societies have this kind of exploitation.

Despite the fact that this kind of exploitation is common and its victims are ordinary people everywhere, this ordinariness is almost universally denied. Sexual abuse in particular is something people don't want to talk about. It's not surprising that most people want to avoid thinking or talking about sexual abuse- it is an ugly, unpleasant, frightening topic. But silence about abuse and denial about how common it is results not in less but in more abuse and exploitation. We may believe that by not talking about it we are avoiding abuse. But the only people who benefit from the silence and widespread avoidance of the topic of sexual abuse are the perpetrators of abuse.

This section of the handbook is intended to help people understand what is common about sexual abuse experiences and people's reactions to them. We begin by describing the most frequently observed changes in emotions, awareness, self image, views of others and views of the world, and the nervous system bases for them. While the next few pages of this guide may seem a little technical, we hope it will help you to understand how your body works when it encounters difficult and frightening experiences.

2. The Body-Mind System

Kids at a Dance

In order to understand the way that people are affected by abuse, we need to understand the way that the body-mind works as an integrated system. Language about the mind and body confuses us into thinking that somehow they are separate things. In fact, the mind and body are so completely integrated that each seamlessly shapes and affects the other. To emphasize that the mind and body are not separate from one another, this guide will use the term body-mind to describe the way they work. To understand how the body-mind system works, let's follow the story of one girl's experience attending a dance performance.

Three Level Brain Diagram

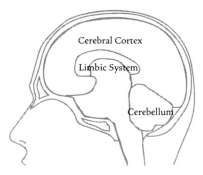

Our girl, Cathy, walks with her friends to the place where a folk dance will take place. She is chatting happily and wearing her favorite, royal blue dress. She is a little excited. Walking to the dance, her brain stem and primary perceptual areas are very active, coordinating the movements of her muscles, her breathing, her heart rate and all the different parts of her body that keep her alive. The lower brain and brain stem is the most basic and essential portion of our brain. The lower brain is just above the brain stem. The brain stem is like a large bulb in the lower back region of the brain. The bulb's stem faces down connecting into the spinal cord. (see diagram) The brain stem is found in all creatures with backbones. We literally can't live without it.

The next layer up of the girl's brain, the *limbic system*, is also moderately activated. The *limbic* is part of the sympathetic nervous system response. The sympathetic nervous system response involves the parts of the brain and other nervous system structures that help us to manage our level of alertness, readiness for action, and for awareness. Going to an event that she expects will be pleasant and interesting activates Cathy's sympathetic nervous system. The girl's eyes are open, she feels very awake. She is listening for interesting sounds, like music. She is looking for familiar and unfamiliar sights, like colorful costumes and light. Her heart rate and breathing will be a little faster than if she were resting quietly at home. Her *limbic system* is mildly activated, and if she is anticipating pleasure, she will interpret her quicker pulse, curiosity, mild muscle tension, and alertness as excitement.

Her interpretation, or the type of experience that Cathy is expecting, is very important. When we note physical sensations like muscle tension, breathing and heart rate, arousal and adrenaline rushes, whether we consider those sensations pleasurable or frightening has everything to do with the next, third layer of our brain. As everyone who has ever taken a ride on a roller coaster knows, whether sensations of excitement are signals of fun or signals of fear is all in our interpretation.

The third layer, the *cerebrum,* and its analytical outer portion, the *cortex,* are the areas of the brain where we process sensations coming from outside and inside our bodies and interpret them so that they literally "make sense". Most processing of sensations is not conscious. In other words, we are not aware of and can't explain most of the cues that we use to interpret our experiences. Ask a girl going to a dance how she is feeling and why, and she will only be able to tell you a small portion of what she is sensing. Cathy may tell you that she loves dances, that she enjoys being with her friends. She may say she is excited, she may even notice that her heart is beating fast. But she is not likely to be aware of most of the specific physical cues that signal that she is "excited". This kind of partial awareness is natural and necessary. If we had to be conscious of every bit of information our brain processed at all times, we would not be able to function in the world. Our brains are literally always receiving too much information for us to manage consciously.

Our minds are biologically programmed, *and* we learn tricks throughout our lives so that we can select the information that is most likely to be important to us. Our nervous systems are both "hard wired" from birth, *and* our experiences continually shape the "software" of our minds through learning. Our brains constantly select information, and very few of the choices of that selection process are conscious. The thoughts we think and the sensations we attend to have a powerful affect on the way that our body sensations "speak" to us. When we learn to use our attention skillfully, we can have more control over our interpretations.

Cathy arrives and stands with her friends around the edges of the dance floor. This dance begins with a performance by a folk dance troupe dressed in bright costumes, moving to lively music from a drum and pipes. The dances and tunes are familiar, based upon traditions from different areas around the country. Our girl's sympathetic nervous system arousal level rises; she is moving to an even higher level of awareness and excitement.

The familiarity of the tunes and dances makes the excitement especially pleasurable. The girl's body and imagination recall other times when she has seen and danced these dances. Cathy finds herself swaying to some of the rhythms, imagining that she has joined the dancing on the floor. After a couple of numbers, the musicians strike up a tune that everyone recognizes as a popular line dance that everyone can join. The dance troupe opens out to the audience and people begin to gather into the line. Cathy, in her royal blue dress, joins the line, wrapping her arms around two other dancers' shoulders; her body moves into the familiar steps. At this stage she has entered into an even higher level of sympathetic nervous system arousal. The dance steps don't require conscious thought; she has known them since early childhood. The music and the steps are interwoven in her memory, so all she needs to do is join the line and the dance steps come out of her feet. Her brain stem is responding to cues from the sensory processing portion of her cerebrum and without thinking, she reproduces a dance step she has learned and practiced in the past.

Up to this point in our story, the process of the girl's body-mind arousal and response is familiar, pleasant, exciting, and pleasurable. When nothing unexpected or frightening happens, an experience is likely to be remembered as fun and enjoyable. Cathy has managed the body-mind information she has experienced smoothly. On both conscious and unconscious levels, her sensations have stayed within a range that she interprets positively. It would be wonderful if all stories were like this and ended happily ever after. But sometimes stories go in a different direction.

When Abuse Occurs:

Let's say Cathy is young, maybe twelve. She is a budding beauty and excited about the first signs her body shows that she is becoming a woman. As she dances, her face flushes, her heart beats and her smile shines with pleasure. She catches the attention of a twenty two year old young man in the crowd, Mikal. They know each other. Mikal is Cathy's cousin and he has watched her growing up. Their families regularly visit with one another and the girl considers the young man part of her family. She is not surprised or uncomfortable when he comes up and says hello to her in the crowd around the dance floor after the line dance. Her breath and heart rate is slowing again after the effort of the dance and she smiles at her cousin. Mikal stands next to her through the last few dance numbers and then, at the end of the performance suggests that he can walk her home.

Because Mikal is her cousin, Cathy is comfortable; she calls him "big brother". Her other friends walk just ahead of the pair. Because her expectations are positive, the girls' level of sympathetic nervous system arousal continues to be moderate. She chats with him easily, not really watching where they are going. It is not until she has followed him down a street she doesn't know and discovers that they are alone in an unfamiliar neighborhood that her brain begins to signal concern. It is not until he pulls her into a deserted dark corner and begins to try to hug and hold her tightly to him that her limbic system lights up with alarm.

At this point, a cascade of chemical and electrical information in Cathy's brain turns on and her body reactions rise to fear. She suddenly feels very afraid, her brain's interpretation of her body sensations has quickly changed. The level of arousal she experiences signals that this situation may be a life threatening emergency. The limbic brain cannot rationally analyze what kind of a danger or emergency it faces. The limbic system perceives serious threats based on pre-programmed criteria, most of which operate outside of consciousness. If those perceptual criteria signal very grave harm, or a potential threat to life, the third, upper portion of the brain is cut out of the information processing cycle. Initially, the brain does not "waste time" thinking through the nature of the threat or the best ways to avoid it. Grave threats are met with pre-programmed body-mind responses that have been designed over millennia of human evolution to help us protect ourselves as organisms. These responses take place at the highest levels of sympathetic nervous system response and are very strong versions of the normal levels of arousal we just described at the dance. The major difference now is that if the body-mind judges that the threat is especially serious, the conscious mind may become partly disengaged from the decision making process.

Our body-mind is programmed under conditions of threat to get ready to fight, to flee, or to freeze. Which of these responses is initiated first is not something we choose consciously. In any given situation and for any person, any of the three responses may occur, this is largely unpredictable. Our brain software makes the choice for us. When our sympathetic nervous system operates at a maximum level of arousal, our body prepares to fight off a tiger jumping out of the bushes, or to run from it, or to freeze in place like a rabbit, hoping the tiger will not see us.

The threat may pass quickly. Perhaps the girl fights, pushes her cousin away and hisses:

"No! I don't want you to do that!"

If the cousin responds by hearing her objection, pulling back and apologizing:

"Sorry, I guess I wasn't thinking. Don't worry, I won't try to make you do something you don't want to do."

The incident may end this way with nothing more than some fear and embarrassment on the part of the girl and the young man. If the two of them learn a lesson from this situation, there may be no lasting harm done.

On the other hand, the young man may push past the girl's resistance. Or perhaps instead of fighting, the girl may freeze and the young man may not notice her fear, or he may interpret her stillness as agreement. If the incident moves beyond Cathy's initial alarm and Mikal pushes past her refusal. If Cathy interprets his behavior as harmful, shameful, embarrassing, or morally wrong, the incident has become abusive. The point where Mikal's behavior becomes abusive is when he pushes past the boundaries of Cathy's comfort or sense of personal choice.

It should be clear here that the imbalance of power between these two people is a key factor in this interaction. If the girl feels strong or powerful enough to say "no" *and if Mikal respects her "no"*, the interaction has not become abusive. Abuse is the misuse of power by one person over another. Mikal is threatening abuse as soon as he takes advantage of Cathy's trust. However, as long as Cathy is able to question Mikal's actions and get a respectful response from him, the line to abuse may not have been crossed. If Mikal stops, this signals that Cathy has the power to influence his actions toward her. When Cathy remains in control of her body and the boundaries of the interaction, her body-mind system can manage the emotional information it is getting and eventually balance and soothe itself back to calmness.

When Cathy cannot assert her own personal boundary, when she cannot say no and her refusal is not respected, she has been violated. That violation of boundaries is sometimes difficult to perceive and to communicate. The sensations involved in such a complicated interaction, one with physical, emotional, moral, intellectual and relational elements, are not always easy to sort out and interpret. The limbic system will be highly activated by a sense of threat. Perhaps Cathy is frightened of being physically harmed; Mikal might say he will hurt her if she doesn't submit. Perhaps she is afraid of emotional hurt; Mikal was a person she thought she could trust to take care of her. But her trust is being betrayed; this is dangerous behavior. She may have moral fears. What will her parents, friends, or others think of her if she submits to Mikal's desires? She may have had expectations or hopes for her romantic life that are violated by this experience. Perhaps Cathy wanted her first physical love to be with a husband.

There are many potential areas of fear, concern or confusion. In fact, if the incident is frightening or confusing enough, Cathy's brain processing capacity may be overwhelmed. It is common for a person facing a boundary threat like this one to have so many "feelings", sensations and thoughts, that the person is literally unable to process them all. At that point, the body-mind system, which cannot stop receiving information from inside and outside sources, begins to "set information aside". What the brain cannot process immediately, it stores for future processing. This is a useful, effective defense under most circumstances.

When abuse occurs, a girl or woman has to cope in the moment by setting aside some of her "feelings". There are times when she has to ignore some of the complicated, confusing, difficult to interpret parts of her experience, and just get through it. Most of the time, our girl will eventually completely recover her body-mind balance. Especially when she has supportive, encouraging friends to talk to, or if she finds reassurance and soothing, she can "catch up" on the postponed body-mind processing. In the best possible scenario, Cathy will cope through the experience, then return to her ordinary life, spend time with supportive friends, and soothe herself. Longer lasting problems, what we call "trauma effects" occur in a small percentage of situations of abuse. Unfortunately, though long term trauma effects are relatively infrequent, they can be devastating.

One of the key points here is that abuse is not especially unusual. Most of the time, the uncomfortable emotional and psychological effects of abuse can be managed and soothed over time. Ordinary supportive relationships, without any special interventions, are enough to help most of us recover most of the time. People are remarkably resilient and capable of recovery, even after very difficult experiences. However, though the majority of people will recover well, there are some people who do not recover quickly or easily. Let's look more closely first at immediate emotional effects of abuse experiences and then consider situations where trauma effects occur and when recovery becomes more difficult.

3. Immediate Emotional Effects

Fear, Anger and Sadness

After an abuse experience, the first things most survivors notice are changes in their emotions. The way that a survivor usually notices emotions is through "feelings" or body sensations. Emotions are basically body/mind experiences of energy and our interpretations of them. As we saw in the story of Cathy, people build perceptions of emotion out of body sensations and interpretations of those sensations.

The most common experience after a frightening incident is **persistent fear or anxiety.** Usually, the fear is directly associated with people, places and things that remind us of the incident. Someone who has been frightened usually does not want to return to the place where the incident occurred or even to places nearby. They may want to avoid thoughts, or anything else that reminds them of the frightening incident. A desire to avoid everything having to do with fear is natural, and in the short run it is not a problem. A survivor may not want to talk about the incident. A period of avoidance is perfectly OK. This is part soothing oneself. But if the avoidance goes on more than a few weeks after the actual danger is no longer present, there is a risk that the fear has entered a self reinforcing cycle and avoidance has become a habit. When fear continues at a significant level, well after the real danger is gone, it is no longer a helpful defense.

Anxiety expresses itself very commonly in muscle tension, elevated heart rate, persistent thoughts about frightening or unpleasant things, and sleep disturbances. A survivor may frequently find herself having memories, thoughts or even nightmares about the bad experience. If these symptoms continue for a few days, even up to a couple of weeks, there is nothing to be alarmed about. Take steps to relax, engage in normally pleasant activities, try to exercise moderately and eat in a healthy way. If in time sleep patterns and physical symptoms return to normal, this is a sign that the body-mind system is processing the experience and healing is taking place.

Some people feel a need to talk about the frightening experience; some people do not. Talking is not essential. But a problem may be developing if sleep and body symptoms do not return to normal and fear persists for several weeks after the real danger is gone. If a survivor's anxiety gets stuck in a pattern of continued avoidance of things associated with the frightening experience, or if symptoms have not begun to improve after about four weeks, it is important to seek additional support. If these symptoms are serious and persistent, professional help may be necessary.

Sometimes after an abuse experience a person may not be aware that they are feeling anxious or fearful. Instead what they may notice, or other people around them may notice, is **irritability or anger.** A person who has been abused may notice that they are having more trouble than usual managing anger, or frustration. Irritability may get out of hand and a survivor may blow up about little issues or have unusually big reactions to things that would not ordinarily seem so significant.

Sadness is another common feeling that may be noticeable after abuse. Feelings of loss or grief may be very strong. For some survivors this emotion may be especially hard to cope with. They may have crying spells, or feel overwhelmed with sadness or despair. Sometimes survivors notice that they are unusually tired or fatigued. A survivor may be aware of a specific loss that they are mourning: lost innocence, loss of a relationship or of an important friend. But sometimes the sadness is not clearly attached to any particular loss. Sadness may feel very broad or general.

Problems Regulating Emotions

What all these emotional changes have in common is that they represent difficulty managing and regulating body-mind responses to events. Abuse experiences appear to throw off a person's emotional balance. Balanced emotional energy and expression can become much harder to regain and maintain. One of the main tasks of our brain, and of our body-mind as a whole, is to help us to maintain a healthy, dynamic balance of energy. It is as if abuse experiences disrupt that energy flow. Healing involves restoring the healthy, balanced flow of energy into, within and through us. Of course living well does not mean being happy, comfortable, or at ease all the time. Ordinary life is full of challenges. But we do have to be able to cope with the natural ebb and flow of our sensations, our emotions and our interpretations. The intensity of our emotions needs to stay within a range that allows flexible functioning.

Sympathetic Nervous System   Parasympathetic Nervous System

The **sympathetic nervous system** response of the body-mind, described in Cathy's story, is one half of a balancing mechanism in all of us called the **autonomic nervous system**. The awakening, activating function of the sympathetic nervous system is designed to work in balance with the **parasympathetic nervous system**. The parasympathetic provides a relaxing, calming, soothing response to external and internal stimuli. (It also promotes digestion, a function that is not necessary during a high stress, short lived attack.)

When Cathy returns home after her experiences, she would be likely to try to rest and soothe herself, perhaps to sleep or relax. The sympathetic and parasympathetic mechanisms function in a dynamic dance, keeping us just awake and alert enough to perform the tasks of life, and then calm and comfortable enough to breathe deeply, digest food and function effectively over a lifetime. All living organisms maintain a functional balance between activity and rest.

A good metaphor for humans' dynamic balance is breath. Both the in breath that brings air into our bodies, and the out breath that releases the gases we don't need back into our environment, are necessary. If we only breathed in or if we only breathed out, we would die. This rhythm in and out is the essence of our lives. One side of the balance cannot be sustained without the other.

When a healthy girl or woman has only one abusive experience it is likely that her resilience will be high. Especially if a survivor is supported, she can recover quickly. If her friends and family believe her story, if they encourage her to soothe herself and take steps to regain balance, she is likely to bounce back to health. She may be able to learn valuable lessons from the experience and then move on.

After sexual abuse most survivors need to take action to protect themselves. Sometimes action is required to protect other potential victims as well. Health care interventions are usually important. There are times when a survivor may choose to take legal actions as well. Health care and legal decisions are complicated and we will consider those parts of the healing process in the third section of this handbook. For right now, it is helpful to remember that a single, relatively uncomplicated experience of sexual abuse may not require a large set of responses to heal. The most important thing is that a survivor be allowed time and be given support to sort out what she needs after abuse or exploitation. It is often not immediately obvious what particular steps an individual survivor needs to take. Taking time and creating safety so that she can sort things out is excellent for calming the body-mind emotional storm that abuse may have awakened.

As we described earlier, the key factor that pushes an interaction over the line from difficult to abusive is the removal of a girl or woman's ability to protect and choose her own boundaries. Healing will involve helping her to regain her sense of power and control over herself. It cannot be overstated that healing from abuse is based upon regaining a sense of the ability to choose and care for oneself. Other people, even close family and friends, should not completely take over and direct the recovery of a survivor. Reclaiming the ability to decide what she wants and needs is at the core of a survivor's recovery.

4. Complicating Factors

Let's consider the factors that tend to complicate abuse experiences. These factors may lead to more severe reactions or to trauma effects that last longer than usual. Ordinarily, trauma reactions last up to about three months after an event, and gradually disappear as the survivor's mind and body heal. Complicating factors may contribute to reactions that last more than three months, in severe situations trauma effects can last many years, even a lifetime.

The story of Ayshe at the beginning of this section illustrates a common pattern for complicated abuse. Ayshe is vulnerable to more trauma effects for several reasons. First, Ayshe was very young when she was first abused, six years old. Second, the abuse continued for a period of years. Third, the abuser was a person Ayshe considered part of her trusted family; her trust was violated. Fourth, Ayshe was too afraid to tell anyone about her abuse. She kept the secret over many years with a growing feeling of shame and self-blame. For all of these reasons, Ayshe is at risk for more complications and a serious psychological reaction to her abuse.

1. Age and Development:

When children are abused, their age and stage of biological, psychological and social development affects their response to the experience. The younger a child is when the abuse begins, the more likely it is that the abuse will impact the pattern of her relationships, thoughts and emotions over a long time. There are particular stages of children's development that are especially important for building relationship skills, trust, coping and emotional soothing. A complete discussion of the impact of age and developmental stages is beyond the scope of this handbook. But it is important to note that the age factor is quite important for understanding abuse effects, especially for young survivors.

For example, at six years old Ayshe is in a vulnerable stage of her development. She is learning psychological skills for trusting others. She is learning to believe in herself and in her ability to do things competently and effectively. Six year olds practice all of these very basic psychological lessons. Through abuse Ayshe experiences a deep violation of her trust. Abuse may confuse her ability to identify what she needs. It disrupts her ability to practice making choices about what she wants and needs. If she is unable to discover and act upon what is best for her, Ayshe may have problems developing basic confidence and interpersonal skills.

This is a complex topic and we can only mention it here. Remember, age is significant because of the way it affects psycho-social development. Development occurs at different rates for different people, but the broad patterns are universal. Abuse can have significant affects on psychological and social development.

2. Repeated Occurrence:

Remember what makes a roller coaster fun or frightening? Our interpretations, our expectations, and the way that we make sense of experience, all are extremely important. There is no objective way to measure the subjective experience of repeated violations of trust. For instance, the effects of sexual abuse may be intensified in the context of constant criticism, or when accompanied by physical violence, or when they are connected with other frightening experiences. Survivors who experience abuse repeatedly, especially if that abuse begins at an early age, are at higher risk for complications and traumatic effects after the abuse.

It makes common sense that when a harmful experience occurs more than once, it will have a different impact than a single incident. When an experience is repeated, it is reinforced, we learn. Thoughts and feelings that occur again and again have a strong impact on a person's understanding of the world. Repetition may occur in the form of similar or of different types of abuse- emotional, physical or sexual. A survivor is the person who can perceive whether the abuse is repeated. It makes a difference if she perceives herself to have been a victim multiple times, and if she connects her experiences into a pattern of abuse.

3. Relationship to the Abuser:

The relationship that a survivor has with her abuser has many effects on the way that she perceives the experience. Naturally, the meaning a survivor assigns to her experience is influenced by the person who abuses her. One very difficult aspect of abuse by a total stranger is the fear it often kindles that no one can be trusted. Every unknown person can seem to be a potential attacker. The world may seem like a very dangerous place, full of unpredictable strangers. Rape or molestation by a stranger may result in a very high level of continuing, generalized anxiety.

On the other hand, if the abuser is a previously close and trusted person in the survivor's life, a friend, a teacher, a doctor or a family member, that loss may feel devastating. If a survivor previously considered the abuser to be her protector, she has lost some of her sense of safety in the world.

Particularly when the abuse takes place within a family, for instance if the abuser is a girl's older brother or her father, the emotional dilemma for the survivor is extremely complicated and confusing. A person that a survivor should be able to trust to protect her has acted to harm her. Sometimes a child's life literally depends on this person. This kind of situation, incest, is very frightening and confusing. A betrayal like this also makes confronting the abuse especially difficult and complicated.

One of the reasons that incest is a particularly devastating type of sexual abuse is because it seriously complicates the task of finding support and safety. The people who should be available to help with soothing and support are also involved in the problem. When telling someone about abuse requires risking a fearful, angry or sad response, a survivor is caught in a dilemma. After she has been frightened, hurt or confused, a survivor needs to calm down. Her sympathetic nervous system arousal needs to be balanced out by parasympathetic soothing and rest. For most people, family members are among the most important sources of emotional soothing and support. Incest creates a situation where people who should be sources of safety in a girl's life, her family, become sources of danger.

4. Finding Safety and Support:

Incest is an extreme example of complications around supportive relationships, but finding safety and support can be complicated for other reasons as well. Sometimes the abuser is not a member of the family but is a member of the family's trusted circle of friends. Sometimes the abuser is a partner, a teacher or a doctor, or someone else that represents the kind of relationship a survivor needs to respect and wants to trust.

Whoever the abuser may have been, whatever the survivors' relationship to him is, she must find safety. Abuse is a profound disruption of a girl or woman's sense of safety. In Ayshe's story, in a relationship or a situation where she expects to be safe, Ayshe has been harmed. To recover from this loss of confidence and trust, she needs to learn to recreate a sense of safety. Sometimes that task is not so difficult. If there are enough supportive people and safe situations available in a survivor's life, she may quickly find ways to feel safe and soothe her body-mind system. If however, supportive people or safe situations are difficult to find, as was the case for Ayshe, recovery may be complicated and trauma effects may become a problem.

Safety is not the same for every person. We will examine more closely how to create a sense of safety in the section on healing. The key point is that each survivor must develop an understanding of herself. She must discover and cultivate the skills of calming and soothing herself. For everyone a first step in soothing involves feeling safe, or safe enough.

It is not unusual for a survivor to have difficulty finding safety after abuse. If the abuser is a parent or a husband, the complications for meeting a girl or woman's basic needs are many and serious. If getting away from sexual abuse would require losing her source of food and shelter, or if a survivor has depended upon the abuser for a home and income, her survival is threatened. Basic survival must be ensured and ensured on a sustainable basis before an abuse survivor can feel completely safe. Complete safety may not be possible. But relative safety, in a form that a survivor can genuinely feel, is essential to recovery.

Once safety or relative safety can be reestablished, a survivor can proceed to do the work of soothing her body-mind reactions. She can re-connect again with people who are trustworthy. She can begin to understand her experience in ways that are helpful to her instead of harmful. Eventually, she can move on and put the abuse behind her. We will talk at more length in the second section about these steps in the healing process. But the point is that safety and support for recovery are fundamental prerequisites to other parts of healing.

When abuse experiences become chronic or when the victim is subjected to a prolonged period of totalitarian control, the consequences much more frequently include trauma effects. An example of this is when a girl or woman is a victim of sustained domestic violence or continued sexual and physical abuse within her family. Also when a girl or woman has been held in organized conditions of sexual exploitation like trafficking or prostitution, she is very likely to experience complex trauma effects.

Chronically abusive situations prevent a girl or woman from reestablishing an ordinary experience of safety. Instead, simply in order to survive, a victim of prolonged or chronic abuse must learn different ways to feel safe, even when real safety is not available. These conditions lead to complicated psychological and emotional adaptations that involve serious psychological distortions.

If a sense of safety can only be created through serious distortions and those distorted adaptations need to be maintained over a significant period of time, say many months or many years, a survivor has altered her body-mind functioning in order to survive. These alterations do not have to be permanent, though with current brain imaging techniques, actual physiological changes have been noted in children who have been severely abused. It is clear that in order to relearn and overcome the effects of chronic, complicated abuse, a longer more sustained process of healing is required.

In the next section on healing we will look in more depth at the process of identifying and developing a sense of safety after abuse. At this point we want to emphasize that to avoid trauma effects or more serious body-mind symptoms after abuse experiences, a girl or woman must be offered support and find safety.

5. Vulnerabilities Before the Abuse:

Another complicating factor that may increase the likelihood of serious effects after abuse are mental illnesses, emotional, or developmental problems that exist before the abuse occurs. We know that mental illness manifests in people who have a combination of biological, environmental and interpersonal vulnerabilities. For instance, if a girl or woman already has problems with depression, anxiety, mood regulation or disordered thoughts before she is abused, the abuse may have more serious results. Resilience, the ability to bounce back from harm, is greatest in people who have the sturdiest biological, psychological and environmental resources. Survivors who begin with a less flexible and varied set of resources before abuse, have less strength to bounce back. Abuse may become the trigger that touches off a problem that was ready to manifest anyway. The body-mind condition of a person before abuse affects the body-mind consequences of abuse. This means that children and women who are more vulnerable need additional protection and support.

In the section below discussing Problems with Consciousness and Thoughts, we will discuss the dissociation defense. A person who tends to split off, "go away" or withdraw awareness as a way of coping before abuse, may find that the habit becomes more problematic afterwards.

6. Perceived Severity of the Abuse

We have deliberately not described details of particular abusive acts as a key complication. For a long time in psychology and in the legal process, there has been an over focus on the details of particular acts of sexual abuse. For instance, there has long been a belief, reflected in many laws, that penetration of the victim's body by another person's organs or other objects, is more damaging than experiences that do not involve penetration of the victim's body. That focus on one detail of a sexual act is a distraction. Penetration or lack of penetration does not make the most important difference in the damage done by sexual exploitation.

The focus on details like penetration is based on an effort to find some "objective" standard for measuring abuse. This focus clearly reflects a natural human wish to be able to rationally measure abuse and the experiences of survivors. The assumption is that if we could measure or rationalize abuse, somehow the suffering involved might be more easily quantified and controlled.

Trauma survivors themselves often get lost in lengthy, obsessive efforts to remember, define or re-capture the details of abuse experiences. The experience of abuse makes a survivor feel so out of control, it is not surprising that she wants to re-establish any sense of control that she can. Sometimes it seems that remembering every detail of abuse might help her to regain control. The problem is that control can never be established over experiences that occurred in the past. Past experiences are in the past and cannot be re-made. What must be established instead is control over our present reactions. After safety in the present is established, real control can occur over the body-mind reactions that have been stirred into a storm by past experiences. Both the survivor of abuse and the people who are her supporters need to keep this in mind.

Of course the specific acts involved in the abuse do have meaning for the survivor. In the process of recovery a survivor will deliberately examine the meanings that the abuse experiences have for her. She will consider ways that she wants to re-frame those experiences into a new narrative. The narrative or the story that she tells herself about the abuse is a powerful part of her interpretation of that experience. Remember the roller coaster? It is very important that the survivor has a sense of control over the story that she tells herself. She also needs to feel control over the story she tells others about what the abuse meant to her. Paradoxically, a survivor's ability to establish a healthy focus and regain some sense of control in the present is the key to the question of the severity of abuse.

Many times survivors are told stories by other people, and often they tell themselves stories about their abuse that distort the severity of the experience. Some factors may become exaggerated and feel worse, but most often survivors minimize the hurt that they have experienced as a result of abuse. Of course helpers want to reassure a survivor. In fact it is quite healthy for a survivor to tell herself calming things about her experiences. But when minimization hides things from a survivor that have real and significant influences on her life, that interpretation is not helpful. We will discuss this "minimization" factor, severity and realistic assessments of the effects of abuse again in the section on healing. The main point for now is that there is no objective measure of the severity of abuse experiences. It is always possible to find someone who has had a more horrific experience, and it is always possible to find someone who seems better off. But ideas about severity are subjective interpretations. Interpretations can change depending on many complicated factors. The severity of psychological damage is nearly impossible to predict based just upon a physical description of an abusive act.

5. Complex Post Traumatic Stress Disorder

When complicating factors add up, it is possible that a survivor of sexual abuse may suffer serious consequences. Particularly if prolonged abuse began in childhood or if a woman lives for many years in an abusive marriage, she may develop a characteristic pattern of symptoms. A team of trauma researchers associated with psychiatrist Judith Herman called this pattern of symptoms "Complex Post Traumatic Stress Disorder." Their descriptive list may be useful for many survivors because it is such a comprehensive overview of symptoms experienced by survivors of many kinds of trauma. Every survivor will not experience all of these symptoms; each person is different. But this list helps describe a range of effects of complex trauma for many survivors. We have paraphrased Herman's more technical list into simpler, less scientific language, more easily understood by general readers. For some people a list of behaviors will be more helpful, so we have also included a second list that describes behaviors rather than symptoms.

Common Responses After Sustained, Serious Abuse [01]

1. Changes In Emotions

- Fear of feelings, situations and experiences associated with the traumatic experience
- Difficulty containing or managing emotions like anger, sadness, fear
- Preoccupation with death- may include suicidal behaviors
- Harming oneself

---

[01] Based upon Herman, J. L. (1992) *Trauma and Recovery*. New York: Basic Books.

- Persistent sadness, fatigue, hopelessness
- Exaggerated or completely suppressed sexual feelings

2. Changes In Awareness

- Repetitive memories, dreams, and fantasies related to the traumatic experience
- Trouble remembering certain times and events associated with the traumatic experience
- Tendency to split off and distance, withdraw or avoid awareness
- Numbness
- Difficulties feeling real or relating to the world as real
- Preoccupation, obsessive thoughts

3. Changes In The Survivor's Feelings About Herself

- Helplessness, passivity, difficulty taking initiative
- Shame, guilt and self blame
- Undervaluing herself or her accomplishments
- Sense of separation, isolation and difference from others- may include a sense of being "special"

4. Changes In The Way The Survivor Sees Others

- Over-focus on and over-attribution of power to the perpetrator
- Idealization or gratitude toward the perpetrator
- Acceptance of the mindset of the perpetrator
- General isolation and withdrawal
- Serious problems developing trust in relationships coupled with an intense desire to make relationships of trust
- Repeated failures to self protect

5. Changes In The Way Survivor Understands The World
- Loss of sustaining faith
- Sense of hopelessness and despair

Common Behaviors of Traumatized Survivors Include:
- Alcohol and drug abuse
- Self injury, cutting, various forms of self harm
- Suicidal feelings and actions
- A pattern of unhealthy relationships with inappropriate partners
- Underachievement or "not living up to her potential"
- Difficulty performing academically or professionally
- Helplessness, depression, fatigue
- Angry outbursts, irritability
- Unstable moods- high highs, low lows
- Unreasonable fears
- Obsessive or compulsive behaviors
- Losing awareness or concentration, difficulty staying present and focused

These lists could be longer. They show a wide range of symptoms and behaviors, and many of these problems can be very serious. It is important to say here that any of these symptoms could be a sign of a wide range of different psychological and emotional problems. Based simply on observations of a few symptoms, one must not assume that a person has experienced trauma. However, sometimes it is helpful for survivors to know which common behaviors may be connected to abuse. Survivors are frequently bothered by particular behaviors but don't know that these behaviors might be connected with their abuse experiences. Knowing that some of these problems will improve with recovery from trauma is often very reassuring. Clearly, recovery that reduces these kinds of distress can have major benefits for survivors.

6. Problems with Consciousness and Thoughts

After complicated trauma a few symptoms occur often enough that it makes sense to describe them here. Sometimes these trauma effects can be alarming for the survivor and to her supporters. It may be helpful to know that these symptoms are often considered effects of complicated sexual abuse.

Survivors, as we mentioned earlier, often have periods of anxiety and depression. Difficulties with concentration and memory are common signs of depression or anxiety. It is also not unusual for survivors to have thoughts, memories, or dreams about traumatic events or things related to them. Those thoughts, memories or dreams may be very vivid. They may intrude during ordinary life and may even be powerful enough to make a survivor feel as if she is suddenly re-living the traumatic experience. These kinds of intrusive thoughts, memories, dreams or nightmares usually subside with time. But they can be distracting, disturbing and intense.

Another common problem with thoughts for many survivors is getting stuck on certain ideas or feelings. Repetitive thoughts may preoccupy a survivor. She may have a very hard time letting go of certain thoughts or focusing her attention the way she would like to. In the second section on healing we will discuss this kind of obsessive and compulsive thinking and a few things that a survivor can do about them.

Despite the fact that it only occurs in some survivors, one of the alterations in consciousness that can be disturbing for survivors and supporters is disassociation. Disassociation is a change in consciousness that begins as a useful defense during a traumatic experience. When an experience becomes overwhelming emotionally, physically or psychologically, humans have the ability to "step back and away" from it in their minds.

Because our brains constantly receive far more information than our conscious mind is capable of processing, lots of perceptual processes go on outside of our awareness. As we saw with the discussion of Cathy and Mikal at the dance, in an alarming situation, the amount of information can literally become too much to manage. An overwhelming level of body-mind arousal sometimes leads a survivor to protect herself by disconnecting from awareness. When she cannot actually physically get away, sometimes an unconscious body-mind choice may lead her to psychologically 'step away', or disassociate, from an experience. Without knowing what she is doing, a girl or woman may 'go away' from a situation in her mind to reduce the psychological impact of the experience on her in the present. This is actually a great protective strategy and not a problem if it doesn't become too frequent or automatic.

The problem with 'going away', 'splitting', or 'disassociation' is that it can become a habit and that habit can begin to operate automatically, unconsciously. Internal or external cues, frequently unconscious cues, may suddenly trigger a survivor to "go away" from the present in her awareness. She may find herself having trouble following conversations. She may have trouble remembering where she is, or who she is. She may even at times begin to behave like an entirely different person.

There are various ways that disassociation shows up in different people and situations. Many times a person who dissociates frequently can feel as if she is "going crazy". Sometimes a survivor's behavior may make absolutely no sense to an outside observer. Disassociation can even put a survivor into danger.

These kinds of thought distorting symptoms, if they occur frequently or are disrupting a survivor's ability to live her life, are a sign that professional trauma therapy is necessary. This handbook is not designed to treat that level of traumatic distress. If you or someone you care about is having frequent dissociative symptoms, it is important to get them professional psychological help.

7. Problems with Relationships

As we mentioned earlier, some of the most serious problems that sexual abuse causes are in survivors' interpersonal relationships. Healing the destructive patterns and bad habits that sexual abuse can help to create is one of the most important goals of recovery for most survivors. Many survivors are dissatisfied with the quality of their relationships but frequently do not see a connection between their behavior in the present and abuse experiences in their past. Because improving the quality of relationships is the central theme of this guide, we will return to this topic again and again in many forms. But let's list some of the most common relationship challenges that survivors report.

a. Serious Problems with Trust: Survivors report both an intense desire to trust and find trustworthy people and often at the same time, deep mistrust and difficulty trusting anyone. This may play out in looking for a rescuer or a person who the survivor can depend upon, alternating with great disappointment in the normal mistakes and shortcomings of ordinary people.

b. "Bad Radar": Survivors often remark upon the difficulty they have with choosing good, trustworthy friends or intimates. Many trauma survivors appear to develop a habit of selecting people who repeat the hurtful habits or behaviors of earlier abusive relationships. It is as if their "radar is broken" for early signs of trouble in others.

c. Poor Self Image: It is extremely common for survivors to underestimate their own value or accomplishments. Many survivors have unrealistically low estimates of their own abilities or they do not see their successes as significant. This contributes to choosing friends and intimates who may not be worthy of them.

59

d. Isolation and Withdrawal: Survivors may become socially isolated and withdrawn from others. There are a variety of reasons that survivors cite for this including: difficulty with trusting or feeling disappointed in others, feeling different or separate from others, shame, social stigma and embarrassment, fear of judgment or disapproval from others, fear of getting close because closeness has become associated with harm.

e. Sexual Problems: Sex and sexuality tend to be complicated and sensitive areas of relationships for everyone. For women who have had sexual abuse experiences, sex and sexuality become even more complicated. There are two major patterns for survivors of sexual abuse. In one pattern, many survivors become hypersexual and may seek out or involve themselves in risky or problematic sexual situations. In the other pattern, many survivors try to avoid sex and sexually involved relationships altogether, perhaps out of fear, shame or other strong feelings. Sometimes a woman may find herself swinging between these extremes. Women may also develop specific problems with their sexual functioning. We will discuss all of these issues in a little more detail in the section on recovery and healing.

There are a large range of symptoms and problems that may be direct effects or may in some way be related to the experience of sexual abuse. Every person is different and every person's way to healing and recovery is also different. But the important thing to remember is that, even though the pain of abuse may be very great, it is always possible to recover. It is never too late to start the recovery process. With safety, support and proper encouragement, anyone can feel much better. Let's turn now to a discussion of healing and recovery.

PART II

The Recovery Process: How Do We Heal?

1. Finding Safety

Recovery from abuse, and healing after traumatic experiences is not only possible, it is likely. Most people who experience trauma gradually overcome most of their body-mind symptoms and live good lives. Many people do not need formal therapy. However, the problem is that while survivors are usually able to find ways to cope and function even if they never focus directly on healing, their functioning is often more inflexible and less satisfying than if the survivor had never experienced abuse. After a full healing process, a survivor may emerge more capable, more satisfied, and more confident in herself and her relationships than if she had never been abused and gone through recovery. Of course there is nothing good about abuse. But healing and recovery can add depth and strength to a person's life that was not there before. Full recovery and healing offer survivors powerful benefits.

Recovery and healing from traumatic experiences, like the problematic reactions to abuse, follows a fairly predictable process. When an abuse experience is recent or very complicated, it is often difficult to imagine finding a clear path to recovery. This guide lays out some steps that have been useful to many people under a wide range of circumstances. Each survivor will have a unique recovery process. No two survivors are the same before the abuse, no two situations are identical, and no two recoveries will be exactly the same either. But we can identify steps that help many people with healing and recovery.

Healing Stories

Bonnie was sexually abused by her older brother for three years when she was between eleven and thirteen years old. She never told anyone but her younger sister. She was afraid of how her family might react and she felt ashamed. Her sister kept the secret and Bonnie liked to think that she might have protected her sister from similar abuse by warning her about their older brother. Bonnie dropped out of school part way through middle school. Her grades had been getting worse since the fifth grade when the abuse began. Eventually, school seemed too difficult, though she had done well in primary school. The abuse ended when Bonnie's brother left to do his military service. By the time her brother returned, Bonnie was married and had gone to live in her new husband's household.

Bonnie married Adam because her family chose him for her. She didn't dislike him at first, but as time when on, she discovered that Adam had problems with his moods. He was easily frustrated and irritable, and after he took a job under a boss who was harsh and critical, Adam began to lash out verbally at Bonnie. He was angry that she didn't want to have sex with him whenever he was in the mood. It wasn't long before he began to hit her when he was upset about problems at work. Bonnie tried hard to be a good wife and make the household comfortable for Adam. She cleaned and cooked and took care of their two small children. But Adam was never satisfied. The physical beatings got worse as Adam began to drink alcohol, trying to manage the dark moods that came over him more and more frequently.

One day, Adam slapped Bonnie so hard that she fell, hit her head on a table edge and broke her jaw. When Bonnie came back to consciousness, she was looking into the tearful face of her eleven-year-old daughter. At that moment, something snapped in her, and Bonnie decided things had to change. She found out about a women's support center where there were groups for women trying to recover from abuse. She began to visit the center during the day when the children were in school and Adam was away at work.

At the women's center Bonnie felt safe. She learned that the beautiful openwork tablecloths her mother taught her to make could bring a good price from a women's co-operative sales program. She expanded her skills to other products and began to make a little money for herself. She also learned some things about her legal rights and realized that it was not acceptable for Adam to hit her. She began to leave the house whenever he came home drunk, taking her children with her to a friendly neighbor. After Adam had fallen asleep, Bonnie and the children would return home. A counselor at the women's center also taught her some body-mind skills to help Bonnie calm herself down when she got frightened. Bonnie taught those skills to her children as well.

Adam was angry that Bonnie was becoming more independent, but she didn't back down. More and more often she left the house when he began to threaten her. One day she even went to the local police station and made a complaint after he came home drunk and hit her again. Adam's brother and father spoke with Adam and told him that his behavior was embarrassing the family. They began to look for a new job for him, hoping that Adam would do better with a different boss. This support from Adam's family really helped the situation; Bonnie felt stronger and Adam began to feel a little more hopeful.

One of the best things that happened was that Bonnie found out about a scholarship program. The women's center helped Bonnie's daughter to get a scholarship so that she could go to the science high school. The whole family was proud of her success and Bonnie knew that standing up for herself was helping her daughter to succeed too. Bonnie was on a path to healing, helping herself and her family.

Body-Mind Healing

As described in Bonnie's story, the first step to calming and soothing the body-mind is finding safety. Bonnie began her recovery the moment she "snapped" and started looking for support. Bonnie was fortunate and found a women's support center. Through the center, she began to participate in activities that helped her to feel stronger and more confident. Once she had this safe place for learning, she began to practice the new skills that could help her to feel better. As Bonnie found support, she began to work on establishing both internal body-mind safety and external life situation safety. Inner and outer safety are separate, but intertwined.

What is Internal Safety?

Finding and establishing safety involves two levels of work, external and internal. External safety depends on making sure that a survivor's practical situation is secure and protected. A girl or woman who is afraid for her survival cannot do the important work of learning how to manage her internal body-mind balance. To have real safety, a woman must have a safe, secure place to live and learn. And she must also develop skills to soothe and manage her internal, subjective body-mind states. In this section, we will focus most closely on the internal body-mind aspect of safety. The external, practical issues are just as important and will be addressed more fully in the third section of this handbook. A survivor needs other people like friends, advocates and professional service providers to help her address many external safety factors. We mention both because internal and external factors influence one another. However, this section is focused on what a survivor can do best for herself.

As we described in the story of the kids at a dance, abuse disrupts a person's body-mind balance. The sympathetic nervous system response that naturally creates physical readiness to fight, flee, or freeze, gets stuck. When instead of a sudden, short-lived attack we experience extended threats, long-term stress, or painful, complicated emotions, the sympathetic nervous system may activate and stay active. The body-mind may not fully shift back to a strong, balancing parasympathetic response and calm down. When the internal process of soothing and calming ourselves does not happen in a natural, balanced way, we have to learn to use our awareness and thoughts to change the messages to our body-mind. If abuse throws our body-mind balance off, we can use conscious skills to turn down the stress, panic or a sense of threat. We can consciously trigger a reassuring, relaxing response. Once we shift toward soothing ourselves, our body-mind can begin to rest and recharge again.

The Physical Systems Involved In The Autonomic Nervous System Are:

Heart Rate	Urination
Digestion	Sexual arousal
Saliva production	Respiration or breathing rate
Perspiration	Thoughts
Dilation of the pupils	

These nervous system functions are "wired together", which means they operate as an interconnected set of related functions. While strictly speaking thoughts are not a part of the autonomic nervous system, in practice they work with and have a profound effect on the rest of the system. We are discussing thoughts here as part of the autonomic system because conscious and unconscious cues turn all these responses on together.

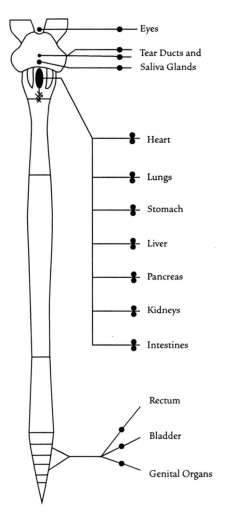

- Autonomic Nervous System -

Most of these mechanisms operate outside of our conscious control most of the time. Together these systems work to maintain a healthy balance, and are designed not to depend upon our conscious control. When our survival is threatened, we cannot think about everything necessary to stay alive. But there are two parts of our autonomic nervous system that we can always deliberately alter: **our thoughts and our breathing.** In other words, the best tools we have for consciously triggering or strengthening our parasympathetic, calming responses are our thoughts and our breathing.

When life is going well and we feel balanced, it is fine for our body mechanisms to operate without awareness. The body is beautifully designed to take good care of itself. Ordinarily, activity and arousal are kept in balance with rest and digestion, and we stay healthy. But abuse, especially prolonged or repeated abuse, tends to throw off the balance and keep our body-mind stressed and uncomfortable. When our balance has been off too long, the body-mind system becomes more fragile, less resilient and less efficient. Our behaviors and thoughts tend to become rigid and habit bound in an effort to protect us. Using skills for conscious body-mind control can help us return to a resilient state. Breathing well and thinking right are important keys to this process.

To create an internal sense of safety, first we must become aware of our distress or acknowledge the anxiety, and begin to communicate more consciously with our own body-mind. We can begin to use breath and thoughts to signal to our body-mind that the stress we feel is not a threat to our survival. We are signaling to our nervous system that there are no tigers jumping out of the bushes to kill us. To create internal safety, we need to learn skills for soothing ourselves and activating a balancing, calming parasympathetic nervous system response. Let's examine those skills step by step. We begin with understanding thoughts and feelings about safety.

Creating Internal Safety

What is safety? The answer to that question may not be as obvious as it first appears. We each have a unique temperament and set of experiences that shapes us. Our personal sense of safety is built out of unique interpretations from our own experiences. Something that seems safe and comfortable for one person may seem risky and dangerous to another. For instance, some of us feel most safe when we are in a quiet, still place; some of us feel soothed by noise and activity. Some people feel calmest around other people; others prefer being alone and turning inward. There are a huge number of variables that may contribute to a survivor's sense of safety.

A survivor can explore her own feelings of safety. She must identify what she needs to do for herself to increase her personal sense of safety. She may need help with some of the tasks involved in building external safety. But no matter what her external situation is, a survivor can always reflect upon the things that are most likely to reassure, calm and soothe her. Other people can share ideas with a survivor about what helps them, but because every person is different, other people can only suggest; a survivor must discover her own unique formula for feeling safe. Here is an exercise for working with thoughts on finding safety.

TRY THIS

Steps to Finding Safety

1. **Talk with friends and supporters.** Ask others what helps them; some of these things may also help you. It is best to talk with several people so that you can hear a range of different types of coping and safety measures. Ask them what safety means to them. What do they like to do to feel safe? Take an informal survey.

2. **Reflect and remember.** There have been times in the past when you felt especially safe. If it is hard to remember a clear feeling of safety, think about times that have been a little bit safer than usual. Remember the circumstances in your life that have been most comforting and calming. What have you done at different times and under different conditions to soothe and comfort yourself?

If you cannot remember soothing or comforting yourself, what do you tend to do instinctively when you want to comfort someone else? These memories and instinctive urges can be called up in your imagination. Memories and daydreams are also a guide for you. They give you information about yourself.

3. **Experiment.** Try some things out that have been suggested by others or by your own intuitive urges. Try several things. Try things that you have done before and that have been helpful, but also try a few new things. Don't automatically reject an idea because it is new or seems strange to you. Experiment with yourself.

You will discover that you are better off if you have a variety of different tools. The more different choices you can exercise to help yourself to feel safe or to calm and soothe yourself, the better. No tool will always be available. Nothing will work every single time. So have other things to try if one of your usual comfort methods is not available or if it doesn't work.

4. **Look inside and outside yourself.** After being abused, some girls or women become intensely focused on trying to control the circumstances outside and around them, hoping to feel safer. For instance, a survivor may obsessively lock doors. If she is a mother, she may become overprotective of her own children. She may compulsively clean her house. Once a survivor is in a basically secure situation, when the locks and windows are repaired, when adequate protection has been put into place, when the abuser is no longer able to threaten her, she must look at herself. Eventually, survivors' efforts to

control outside circumstances do not offer a lasting feeling of safety. Once basic security is established, safety must be created inside the survivor herself.

TRY THIS

Full Body Breath

Thoughts and behaviors are one important part of finding a sense of safety. Another key factor is breath. Here is a simple exercise for using breath to soothe yourself. Often long after the external threat is gone, our body-mind system is still reacting as if the threat were right beside us. The sympathetic nervous system response has become stuck in "red alert". Our breath is often high in the chest, shallow and tight. That breath may not shift until we convincingly signal to our body-mind that the danger is past. Our parasympathetic breath response may have become dampened or disabled. Turning inward consciously and signaling with breath to the body that the emergency is past is part of self-soothing. Here are some steps you can use to soothe yourself with breath.

1. **Go to a secure place.** First go to a place where the external circumstances feel reasonably secure to you. If you prefer being alone, go to a solitary spot. If you like being in a crowded place, sit in a public spot. If you like noise, find it; if you prefer quiet, find that. If you are happiest in natural surroundings by flowing water or under trees, go there. If you have a favorite room or place in a house, go there. Set up the outside circumstances so that you feel secure enough to turn your attention inward.

2. **Make your body comfortable.** Sit or lie down. Loosen tight clothing and uncross your legs and arms so that your posture is relaxed and easy. Put your feet flat on the floor or flatten your back to the ground. You should have a sense of being firm, solid and stable.

3. **Close your eyes or un-focus your gaze.** The point of this is to let your attention go inside. If looking at things distracts you, close your eyes. If you prefer open eyes and a soft focus, or perhaps if looking at a special object helps you to turn inward, do that.

4. **Bring your attention to your breath.** Notice the point where your breath comes into your nostrils. Draw in a full, deep breath that goes all the way to the bottom of your belly. Rest one of your hands on your belly gently, and feel it rise as your breath fills you with air. The breath will inflate your belly like a balloon. After swelling with the in breath, your belly will fall again as you breathe out. Pay attention to this rhythmic rising and falling of your hand, the swelling and falling of your soft belly.

5. **Breathe in through your nose and out through your mouth.** Once the rhythm of a full in and out breath is established, your hand on your belly will softly rise and fall. Now, notice the point in your nostrils where each breath comes into your nose and then let the breath flow out softly through your parted lips. You will be breathing in a soft, full body circle. In through your nose, down to the bottom of your belly and then back out again through your mouth. Follow the full circle of your breath with your attention. Hold your attention on this circle of breath for a time.

6. **Notice your body sensations and continue the breath.** For many people, just this attention to a circular, full body breath is helpful. Keep your attention on this rhythm of breathing. Continue as long as you can, gently bringing your attention back to the breath when it wanders away. The goal is just to stay with the breath, nothing fancy, just simple attention to breath.

Automatic Thoughts

One of the most important steps we can take toward better control of our thoughts and emotions is to notice and reflect upon them. For a lot of survivors, thoughts and feelings seem to occur automatically. Most people believe that thoughts and feelings come from somewhere outside of our control and then we have to act upon them. We often believe that our thoughts and feelings "make us do things". For instance, "I can't go down that dark street any more because of a bad thing that happened there." "I am always afraid in bed at night because of bad things that happened when I was in bed." "I was so angry I couldn't control myself, I yelled at them." These are some examples of thoughts and feelings described by survivors.

Every person tends to have automatic thoughts and emotions connected with powerful experiences. This is natural. The problem arises not with the automatic thoughts themselves, but rather when those thoughts are negative, destructive or frightening, and when we feel helpless to affect our thoughts or emotions. In fact, with awareness, we can take a first step toward getting back in control of our automatic thoughts and feelings. If you can notice what you are thinking and the way that those thoughts are connected to feelings, you have taken a big step toward being able to make changes. We may feel helpless in the face of our thoughts and feelings, but we are not. The helpless feeling is in part a result of how little awareness we usually have of our thoughts and emotional process. Start simply by noticing.

TRY THIS

Noticing Thoughts

1. Write down a thought or feeling that troubles you.
2. Notice that it is just a thought. Stand back from your thought or feeling and observe it. Some thoughts or feelings no longer seem as powerful when we put them into words and observe them in a clear light. When you are aware of a thought, you can question it.
3. Put a notebook beside you and do the full body breath exercise. Try writing down some of the thoughts that you notice coming up spontaneously when you sit quietly. These thoughts may be disturbing your feeling of calm or safety, or maybe they are encouraging to you.
4. Don't do anything with these thoughts except write them down and notice them. You don't have to change them or fight them; they are only thoughts. Keep a record of your thoughts as you work on your healing. Notice that they are simply thoughts.

As you move through the recovery process you may be able to use some of these thoughts again. It may be helpful to keep a special notebook to work on the exercises you do with this book. We will come back to the question of how to work with thoughts in the exercise on Facts, Values and Evaluations.

2. Facing the Pain

Memory

One very common automatic thought for survivors of sexual abuse is "I cannot face that pain; it is just too great," or "I will not be able to survive facing that pain, I might go crazy". Often survivors will say: "What good could it do to think about what happened anyway? There is nothing I can do about it. It already happened and I cannot change it." Most survivors report thoughts like these, and there is a clear logic to them. This logic is based upon the fact that at the actual time of the abuse, the survivors' body-mind makes a good, unconscious choice not to think about and feel all the thoughts, feelings and perceptions associated with the difficult event.

Let's go back to the story of Cathy and Mikal at the dance. If an event is traumatic, it is by definition overwhelming. As we saw with Cathy coming back from the dance, ordinary excitement at a social event became a complicated emotional struggle when Mikal crossed the line from trusted friend to someone doing her harm. Suddenly, Cathy had more information than she could process. To protect itself, Cathy's body-mind did not process everything; she set aside some parts of her sensations, thoughts, and memories leaving them outside of awareness. Cathy's body-mind made an unconscious decision that the situation was so dangerous there was not enough time or energy to process all the sensations and thoughts on the spot. Information was stored and set aside for processing later. We want to underline that at the time of the harmful event this is a good, protective strategy.

The problem arises when the protective strategy of postponing processing thoughts, feelings and sensations becomes too rigid or too permanent. Trauma is by definition an event that overwhelms a person's ordinary ability to process and adapt to experience. Normally, experience is managed right away or within a relatively short period of time: minutes, hours or days. But sometimes, overwhelming experiences are set aside or sealed away from awareness with a wall instead of a screen. For various reasons, minutes, hours or days stretch into months and years. Instead of simply putting the processing off until there is enough time, energy and safety, experiences that seem unmanageable are rigidly sealed away from processing, as if forever. This unprocessed un-integrated material can become a problem for the body-mind.

A full discussion of memory and the complex ways that our brain processes information is beyond the scope of this handbook. Scientifically, there is still a lot to learn about the way that memory is built out of the raw information our senses receive, and also about the ways that our minds make sense of that information. But for the purposes of this handbook we will emphasize a few specific qualities of memory.

1. **Memory is built in stages.** Memories begin with taking in information from our environment through our senses. The first filtering happens at this stage. Our senses can only gather some of the information that is present in the world. Humans for instance, can only see light within the "visible range"; infrared and ultraviolet light are outside the range of ordinary perception. A next level of filtering happens as received information is sorted and stored for processing on a short-term basis. Our senses select information, and not every bit of received information is kept over time for processing.

Next, selected information from that short-term store is processed according to biological schemas and psychological patterns that help us to make sense of it and hold it over time in case it is needed. At this stage of processing, sensory information and thoughts are put into an order that makes them part of a meaningful "story". The "story" may or may not be something we are aware of, but stories give meaning and shape to the thoughts, emotions and sensations we are trying to integrate.

Finally, over time, as we use these stories to make sense of more and more experiences, the stories should change or adapt, becoming more complex and inclusive. A story that worked to make sense of some experiences may no longer work for us when new experiences are introduced that do not fit in with that story.

2. **All memory is partial.** Memories cannot tell us the whole truth about any experience. Because memory is built in stages, information is lost and added at each stage. Different people having the same experience process the information from their senses differently and make sense of those experiences through different schemas and filters. Any two people describing the same event will tend to describe it differently.

3. **The "more is more" principle.** The more complicated, intense and emotionally involved an experience is, the more our memories must shape it during processing. Interpersonally traumatic experiences, or situations where abuse of power and trust intrude into ordinary life, are very complex. The stories we shape from them tend to be complex, emotionally involved and connected to some of our most fundamental psychological processes. The following factors increase the complexity of the task of forming a meaningful story about an experience:

- More raw sensory information – an experience rich in sights, sounds and sensations.
- More unusual or extraordinary sensory information – unfamiliar experiences.
- Greater levels of nervous system arousal – when the body-mind is activated more than normal
- An intense level of emotional energy, especially fear, anger or pain

4. **Expectations shape memory.** One of the key factors shaping memory is past experience and expectations. Any new experience must be understood in the light of past experiences. The meaning that we give to any experience depends upon the meaning we gave to previous experiences like it. One of the important things about abuse and interpersonal trauma is that it violates our expectations. Traumatic experience is by definition extraordinary and overwhelming. This factor has very significant implications for sexual abuse, because social habits, norms and culture are very important in forming our expectations about sexuality, trust and social relationships.

Coping and Soothing Ourselves

From this brief discussion of memory I hope it is clear that memory is a process. Memory is not the simple taking in, storing and then reporting of information. We are involved in the process of forming and reshaping memories all the time. To work well with abuse experiences, we need to appreciate how complicated and multi-faceted the processes of memory are. No intense emotional experience is simple to process, the greater the sense of threat to our ordinary way of thinking and feeling and to our sense of bodily safety, the more complicated the memory process is going to be. Memory processes take time and energy and involve changes over time to accommodate new experiences. So it should come as no surprise that the painful memories, thoughts and feelings that are associated with sexual abuse are especially difficult to manage.

Coping is the process by which we manage thoughts, feelings, and sensations. At the times when the processing of an experience like interpersonal abuse or trauma cannot take place smoothly, extra effort is necessary. Trauma survivors need to take time for extra preparation so that their body-mind systems can handle the emotional intensity of remembering and making sense of traumatic events. When we are afraid to face the pain of an abuse experience or memory, we are afraid that we cannot handle the feelings evoked. Like finding safety, coping is a part of healing from abuse that will go better if we have more skills to help ourselves through the difficulties.

Coping and soothing ourselves involves comforting ourselves physically and mentally. The exercises for finding safety in the last section are strategies for signaling to our bodies that it is safe to be calm. Once we have established a basic physical sense of safety, we can work with the thoughts and feelings that disturb us. Next, we will focus on the process of soothing ourselves and coping with thoughts.

Everything is Interpretation; Interpretation is Everything

Because memory is not a pure representation of experience but is always an interpretation, it also remains open to change. The meanings of experiences are formed through the thoughts we have about them. Some of our thoughts are quite conscious and some of them are not. But the key to coping is focusing our conscious attention and interpretations on the kinds of thoughts and feelings that are most likely to help us feel strong or whole. Thoughts that keep us frightened, angry or hurt are usually not helpful. The trick is to bring our interpretations in line with a set of perceptions and choices that can help us to handle our circumstances skillfully and effectively.

One of the big risks with thoughts about complicated events like sexual abuse is that these thoughts tend to distort the experience. Sometimes our thoughts exaggerate the harm; sometimes our beliefs unrealistically minimize the harm. It is possible to interpret a traumatic event in ways that make it feel worse. It is also possible to interpret traumatic events in ways that seem to make things easier but that actually deny important information we need to learn from the event.

Some examples of interpretations that try to *minimize* but are likely to increase damage

•   When a family denies that sexual abuse is going on between family members.

•   When a family blames a girl for the sexual behavior of her older brother toward her.

•   When a father tells a girl that she is immoral or dishonorable after she has been abused by someone older or stronger than herself.

These are examples of interpretations of abuse experiences that are efforts to *minimize* the damage to a family, to blame a girl or to protect an abusive person. These examples are efforts to deny the real impact of abuse.

It is also possible to distort an event in a way that *exaggerates* the problem and increases the risk of harm. For instance, children between the ages of 4 and 7 very often engage in innocent forms of exploratory sex play. It is quite normal for 5 or 6 year old children to be curious about the differences between the bodies of boys and girls, and out of curiosity, to want to look at or to touch one another's private parts. This kind of play is natural and innocent as long as the children are not significantly different in age and there is no force or coercion involved. Natural, harmless sex play is based in curiosity, not in manipulation and exploitation of differences in strength and power.

Unfortunately, adults too often interpret children's behavior in terms of their own fears and ideas about sex. Adults may interpret innocent children's sexual exploration as dangerous or immoral and frighten children away from normal curiosity about and pleasure in their own bodies. Sometimes mothers who have been sexually abused as children can be overly sensitive to this kind of play, because it reminds them of the harm they felt from abuse.

Another common interpretation that *exaggerates* the harm of abuse is to believe that once abuse has occurred, a person can never recover, and/or can never feel well and whole again.

One of the things that we can do to help us test our interpretations of experiences is to talk them over with trusted, impartial, wise friends. Talking over the way we think or feel about events with an intelligent, caring, but not directly involved observer can be a great way to get some perspective on our own thoughts.

TRY THIS

Test Your Version of the Truth

1. **Talk to a good friend.** The trickiest part of this activity is choosing a friend who is trustworthy. Some survivors have been so badly hurt or frightened that they find it difficult to trust anyone at all. Sometimes when the abuse has gone on inside a family, even family members one could usually trust with one's most private thoughts and feelings are connected with the problem. It may be difficult to find a friend who can take an impartial view of the situation. But do your best. Tell this trusted friend the story, or as much of the story of the abuse as you can manage without frightening yourself too much. See what your friend has to say about the thoughts and feelings you describe. Do they tend to interpret the situation the same way that you do, or differently? Does the different interpretation have a "ring of truth" to it? This can be a good "reality check".

2. **Think about different interpretations.** If it is possible to think about your experience in more than one way, try thinking about those different interpretations. Ask yourself if it would make any difference if you thought about the experience differently. Are there any interpretations that you can imagine that would give you more choices or more opportunities to feel strong and good about yourself? Any interpretation that reduces the level of harm to you and to others may be worth considering. But be sure

you are not reducing harm to others by increasing the harm to yourself. That kind of interpretation is not an improvement, it is just a way to keep you down.

3. **Write about your experience.** Especially if it is difficult to find a friend you can trust, or if you just like to write, make some time and space for yourself to write the story down. Start by imagining that you are writing a letter to a close and trusted friend who will accept you no matter what happened. Address the letter to that friend but also know in your own mind that you will not send this version of the letter to anyone. This is a version of the story that can include anything at all. No one should ever see it, so you can say anything you want to say, express everything you can. In the letter tell the story the way you saw it.

4. **Listen to yourself.** Your trusted friend may help you to listen to yourself better, or perhaps writing the story down and hearing yourself talk about the event may point out some thoughts or feelings about the story that you were not aware of before. In your letter put brackets around any thoughts or feelings that are obviously interpretations of the event. Try to become more aware of the meaning that you are giving to the events. Remind yourself that everything is affected by interpretation. Is there any interpretation of events you are using that is harmful to you? What are some alternative thoughts or interpretations? This reflection can be difficult to do alone, so it is best if you can find others to talk your feelings over with. The trauma therapy process often focuses very directly on this part of the work of healing. Many survivors find that the most important benefit they gain from trauma therapy is discovering new ways of interpreting their own experiences. We will come back to this idea of interpretation again in the section called Making a New Story.

Mindfulness and the Here and Now

Anxious or frightened thoughts are common for everyone. Think back to times when you have been anxious or worried. Perhaps you were worried about the outcome of an exam in school and the way that score might affect your future. Most of us have had times when we were upset about something that happened in the past. There are infinite numbers of things to worry about and to fear. But one thing you will notice about anxious thoughts, is that fear and worry are almost always about something in the past or the future. These emotions are almost never focused on something going on right here, right now. Most of the time, right here right now, in this moment, we are OK.

Survivors of sexual abuse are usually not able to do much constructive processing of memories and feelings about the abuse until they are in a relatively calm or stable situation. It isn't advisable to try to face and work through anxieties and emotions about abuse when we are stressed by ongoing circumstances or threats in the present. As we noted before, the unconscious or conscious choice not to focus on and process body-mind information connected with traumatic events is a good, self-protective choice in the middle of a crisis. The body-mind needs a certain amount of basic stability to work through trauma. This process should not be forced. Forced memory and confrontation simply adds new layers of trauma.

Most of us have heard stories from people who went to the police or who tried to confront abuse personally or legally and found that the situation got even worse. This kind of forced confrontation with traumatic pain, without sufficient safety and support is called **secondary trauma.** This kind of additional layer of trauma can be damaging. We will discuss it in more detail in the third section of this guide. The body-mind avoids processing traumatic pain until it feels enough security or safety to cope and manage the challenge. It is intelligent to set up safety and stability so that we have a strong base from which to confront the pain. This is another reason that proper support and sometimes therapy is important to a survivor. Confronting the pain alone may be too overwhelming and unnecessarily add to a survivor's distress.

Once we have enough safety, support and stability around us, we can manage the risk of secondary trauma. Once we can be fairly sure that we will not add new layers of trauma because we are confronting our pain from a weak position, we can focus on the more secure here and now. This is a practice called mindfulness. The practice of mindfulness can be very useful to anyone dealing with anxiety or worry. Two exercises follow that you can use to practice mindfulness and explore what this state of mind is like. While this practice is very simple and should be familiar to all of us, it is also a state of mind that can be difficult to maintain. Mindfulness is very simple, but not at all easy.

TRY THIS

Being in the Here and Now

1. **Sit in a quiet place.** To begin practicing the skill of mindfulness it is usually helpful to be in a quiet place, sitting in comfortable surroundings.

2. **Pick up an ordinary object.** Take an ordinary object in your hand, a spoon, a cushion, or a decorative item. Hold the object in your hand and focus on it. What do you notice about it? How heavy is it? What color is it? What texture does it have? Does it have a smell, a temperature, a shine or a pattern on it of any kind? Notice everything about this object that you can. Pay very close attention to the object; as if you had never seen an object like this before. Touch and feel the object carefully. See it with "new eyes". Feel it with "new fingers". Describe it to yourself as if speaking to someone who has never before seen an object like this.

3. **If you still are having trouble focusing, repeat the activity with a new object.** You can repeat this focusing exercise as many times as you like, until you feel more present and grounded in the here and now.

TRY THIS

5-4-3-2-1 Exercise[02]

Sometimes our thoughts or attention struggle to settle down and focus on the present moment. Sometimes we are so upset or so caught up in a web of troubling thoughts and worries that it seems too difficult to focus our attention and stay in the present moment. You may find that it is not enough to pay close attention to an activity or an object. If you discover that you need more structure to help you concentrate your attention on the here and now, this exercise can be very helpful. It utilizes hypnotic techniques to train attention on the present.

1. **Sit comfortably in a place where you have privacy.** This exercise is best done in a place where you can speak out loud without bothering anyone else. If you do the exercise silently inside your head, it is more difficult to concentrate.

2. **Look around you and name 5 things that you see.** For instance: I see that the wall across from me is painted yellow. I see a couch in front of me. I see the computer screen. I see my own hands on the computer keys. I see that the light from this sunny afternoon is coming through the windows into the room.

3. **Name five things that you can hear.** For instance: I hear the sound of a car going by outside. I hear the buzz of the refrigerator working in

---

[02] Based on the work of Yvonne Dolan.

the kitchen. I hear the sound of my fingers typing this. I hear a car go by outdoors again. (Repetition is fine). I hear someone pounding a nail in an apartment upstairs.

4. **Name five things that you feel, sensations.** For instance: I feel my fingers typing this on the computer keyboard. I feel myself being held up by the chair I am sitting in. I feel some stiffness in my back from sitting and typing a long time. I feel my feet flat on the floor. I feel that it is warm today.

5. **Now go back to the top of the list: Name four things that you see.** I see the computer screen in front of me. I see my fingers moving on the keyboard. I see some papers on the desk behind the computer. I see a pen on the desk beside the computer.

6. Name four things that you hear.

7. Name four things that you feel or sense.

8. Name three things that you see.

9. Name three things that you hear.

10. Name three things that you sense.

11. Name two things that you see.

12. Name two things that you hear.

13. Name two things that you feel or sense.

14. Name one thing that you see.

15. Name one thing that you hear.

16. Name one thing that you feel.

When you have completed this, check in with yourself. How are you doing? Do you need to go back to the top of the list, begin at five again and repeat the activity? If you feel calmer, more focused, maybe you are finished. If you want to repeat the exercise, go ahead and repeat it as many times as you like, until you feel calmer and able to let go of the thoughts and worries that have been bothering you. If you lose your concentration, simply start again wherever you think you may have been in the exercise, it doesn't matter, simply continue.

This exercise requires quite a bit of concentration and the activity makes it difficult to think about other things while we attend to the here and now. Most people find that if they practice this exercise enough, the effect becomes stronger and stronger. With repetition, the body-mind becomes trained to respond to this activity with an increasing degree of relaxation and calm. We recommend that you use this exercise whenever you need to focus your attention away from anxious thoughts, panicky feelings or worries. It can be very powerful and helpful under a wide range of circumstances.

I use the following table to help remind me of the pattern in the exercise;

	5	4	3	2	1
Sights					
Sounds					
Sensations					

3. Building Support and Trust

Blaming the Victim

For survivors, one of the most difficult aspects of the experience of sexual abuse is a terrible feeling of loneliness and isolation. It is as if the experience of sexual abuse, by breaking a bond of trust in our hearts and minds, leaves us feeling that the process of trusting and building relationships is full of unknown dangers. Many survivors want to close up and pull away from other people. They may be afraid that if they take the risk of trusting, they are likely to be hurt again. Perhaps they doubt the possibility of finding trustworthy people. If one of their trusted friends or relatives, or even a complete stranger, turned out to be unexpectedly dangerous, how can they be sure of finding safe relationships?

After sexual abuse there is also often a sense of shame or embarrassment. Other people may blame the survivor instead of her abuser. Traditions like the killing of girls and women when they have been raped or abused are extreme examples of the widespread social habit of blaming the victim. We have all heard stories about victims who spoke up and then were blamed for the abuse. Girls and women may be especially afraid that if anyone knows that they have had sexual experiences, they will be considered impure, dishonorable, dirty, or immoral.

Force and coercion are never the fault of the victim of rape and harassment. We do not bring sexual abuse upon ourselves. Every person who acts on his sexual desires and impulses is responsible for that choice, and it is quite possible for innocent girls and women to be forced or coerced into sex. Blaming the victim is a blatant denial of the privilege and power that males have over females in many societies. Women and girls must not accept this false blame. The shame a victim feels after she has been abused protects no one but the abuser. Abusive people must not be protected, they must be held accountable for their behavior.

When abusive people are held accountable for their bad behavior, they have the opportunity to learn better behavior. When a society holds people responsible for their behavior and expects correction or reparations for wrong action, those actions are much less likely to continue or to be repeated. Unfortunately, around the world, nearly all societies give men privileges over women. In most societies, maleness is favored over femaleness. There are literally thousands of years of tradition and habit that support this state of affairs. There are some societies where inequality and unearned privilege is slowly breaking down. The societies that have been able to make changes in the pattern of male privilege are the societies that have committed to equal human rights through law, enforcement of that law, and systems of accountability for people who break the law.

When a society commits to build equality and then consistently enforces those principles, equality does indeed increase. For instance, "women's representation in elected legislatures in 28 countries now reaches or exceeds 30 percent, widely viewed as the 'critical mass' needed to bring about positive change. Of these countries, at least 23 have adopted quotas or other positive action measures." According to Michele Batchelet, UN Women 2011. It is never easy to change culture deliberately, but cultures all change continuously. Confronting sexual abuse is part of a worldwide culture change that is moving toward greater equality for all people, everywhere. We will talk about this issue more in the final section of this book.

Choosing the Right Friends

When we have had experiences of abuse, we may begin to doubt our ability to choose trustworthy friends. Unfortunately, survivors of abuse sometimes do find that their relationships go badly, over and over again. Very often this is a result of habits learned when abusive relationships began early in a girl's life. Girls who are abused early, by people they should have been able to trust, often do not learn to notice the signs that a person might disrespect or harm them. They often don't feel good enough about themselves to insist upon being respected. Too many survivors do not respect themselves as much as they should and accept mistreatment or disrespect from others because they don't think that they deserve any better.

Even very intelligent, capable and attractive girls and women may believe that they are not worthy or are not good enough to deserve good friends and support. This is very sad and absolutely untrue. This false picture of the self, these fears of being unworthy, broken or immoral are related to the struggle with undeserved self-blame so common among sexual abuse survivors. Distorted, negative self images must be set aside so that survivors can get the trustworthy help and support that they need.

The basic truth is that everyone, no matter what, deserves dignity, help, and encouragement. There is never a good enough reason to deny a survivor the support and help that she needs so that she can learn to build healthy relationships once again. Each person may need to build trust, grow and develop relationship skills at her own pace, and with different kinds of support. But everyone deserves to heal, and all of society benefits from one woman's healing.

So how do we go about choosing trustworthy, true friends? Are there any ways that we can know ahead of time whether a person is likely to be a trustworthy person, someone who will treat us with respect? There are no foolproof tests or perfect ways to know people from our first encounters. Trust always involves a certain amount of risk. But there are ways to increase the likelihood of choosing well. There are some ways to improve our choices of friends. In fact, the most valuable teacher is experience. Using good guidance and then trying out some perceptions will give you an opportunity to learn what trustworthy people are like. The following exercise may give you some ideas about how to choose friends wisely.

TRY THIS

Choosing Your Friends Well

1. **Reflect** on the people you have known and trusted in your lifetime. Review your friends and family members. Who has been a strong, reliable support? Who has done what they said they would do? Who has given you warm, kind friendship and encouragement that you could count on? Who has showed interest for your needs and taken an interest in you? Make a list. Now, think about what those people did that made them trustworthy. What were the particular qualities of the people who have been good to you? They are probably not all the same. There is more than one way to be reliable and more than one kind of valuable support and caring. List the things that have been helpful and useful to you.

2. **Ask your friends.** Ask the people you trust and that have been good to you what they think makes a good friend. Ask them for their ideas about trustworthiness and reliability. Add these ideas to your list of friends' important qualities. List the behaviors that signal trust is safe.

3. **Forgive small mistakes, but don't forget serious errors.** Everyone makes mistakes. The question is - does a person recognize the mistake and learn from errors? If we expect perfection from others, we will always be disappointed. But if we do not hold people accountable to learn from their mistakes, we signal that the mistake is acceptable. Forgiveness allows us and the other person to move on, once an error is recognized and acknowledged. But serious errors may be repeated if we don't make sure to protect ourselves properly. We need to learn who is going to reward our trust with respectful

behavior and efforts to improve. We must recognize who will take improper advantage of trust. This is something we can learn only from experience. We will come back to this issue in the section on social support and accountability. Here is a list to think about when choosing potential friends;

A True Friend Does Not:

- Speak or behave disrespectfully toward you
- Call you names
- Tell you that you are stupid, or unimportant
- Make fun of the things you do to hurt you
- Ignore your requests for considerate treatment
- Frighten you deliberately
- Threaten to do you harm
- Force you to do things that you do not want to do, or that may harm you
- Threaten to harm your children or other things that are important to you
- Threaten to hurt himself if you don't do what he wants you to do
- Treat you as if you are not important
- Be dishonest with you
- Break agreements you make together

This list could go on and would be a little different for every relationship. But these are examples of important problems. Things like this might happen from time to time with anyone. But if you frequently have these kinds of problems in a relationship, you should pay attention, the relationship may be abusive.

4. **Believe what people do, not what they say.** "Action speaks louder than words" is an important truth when dealing with abuse and abusive people. It is part of the cycle of abuse for abusive people to apologize and

93

say that they will not repeat bad behavior. Most people who abuse others know that what they are doing is wrong, but they have not learned to control themselves or to manage their own emotions and behaviors. Abusive people change their behavior only after becoming motivated to make the significant effort to learn new, more respectful, mature behavior. Knowing that abusive behavior is hurtful and unkind is usually not enough to make abusive people stop. Apologies are only a first step toward better behavior. Apologies alone indicate very little. We will come back to the issue of accountability in a later section.

Staying in Charge of Your Own Healing

In this section, we make a clear distinction between children and adults. Children rely on adults to protect and care for them. Of course, every person needs support and care, but children need special support and protection because they cannot make many choices and decisions about what is best for them. The exact time when a person moves from childhood into adulthood, when they gain the necessary maturity to make decisions about meeting their needs, varies from person to person, society to society. Worldwide, legal systems generally designate the eighteenth birthday as the moment when an ordinary, healthy person becomes an adult. For some people and some decisions this seems late, for others this seems early.

If a person is developing well, this birthday will simply be one point on a life long path of increasing responsibility and skill building. The key issue is whether a person has the capacity and the opportunity, with support, to take good care of themselves. Abuse creates difficulties and can distort a person's development so that making good choices, finding the right support, and perceiving healthy opportunities becomes harder. Nonetheless, the goal of every person's development is to discover the best path to feeling as whole and resilient as possible. The healthiest relationships are the relationships that enhance and enrich our wholeness and do not make us feel less worthy or valuable. One person's strength does not need to diminish another's. We can be strong together. The most vibrant communities are the communities where every person's strength and value is encouraged.

From this point of view then, an adult should be the person who makes the important decisions about her own life. Children, on the other hand, must have guidance and informed support to make the best decisions. The balance of care, protection and independence varies from society to society, family to family, person to person. But adults, the world over, should have the legal right and the social opportunity to pursue their own wholeness and healthy lives. Having been a victim of abuse does not mean that a girl or a woman is not able to make decisions for herself. In fact, a survivor of abuse is harmed when she is forced to submit to protections that seriously restrict her activities. If we make it difficult for her to do things for herself, she will be weakened and disabled further by our efforts to "help" her. An adult survivor of sexual abuse needs support and protection so that she can chart a course and define her direction to a good life, by her own standards. Setting goals, recognizing her actual strengths and challenges is very important for healing from abuse.

There is often a temptation on the part of "helpful" people to swoop in and take over from the abuse survivor. It is as if once a mistake in protection has occurred, people want to jump in and do everything possible to "make" the survivor better. But in this rush to "help", people often do not respect or don't fully understand the survivor's needs. A child must be advised and guided. But an adult must be advised, encouraged and then allowed to decide for herself what her healing entails.

If you have experienced sexual abuse, someone has taken advantage of your trust and violated your ability to choose. Healing from sexual abuse involves making new choices for yourself, trusting and being respected.

Though it may be tempting at times to find a "hero" and turn our lives over to someone who can "save" us from life's dangers, none of us lives in a cotton padded box. The world will bring challenges to our door and we cannot be protected from all harm, all the time. Learning to make good choices, learning to trust trustworthy people, learning to build healthy, respectful relationships, and ultimately feeling whole as an adult, involves risks. Beware of helpers who want to take over your life. Unless you are child, you need to make some choices for yourself. Even children need to make some measured choices so that they learn how to choose well. Respect yourself and trust the helpers who treat you with respect. The best help is empowering help. Empowering help makes you feel stronger, more hopeful and capable.

We will talk in later sections about the particular kinds of support a survivor may need from professional helpers and services. The important thing to remember is that every survivor needs a network of support. It takes a good community to bring us back to health after a traumatic experience of abuse. We will talk more about how to build that network in the last sections of this handbook.

4. Making a New Story

Interpreting Again

Let's look once again at the idea that everything is interpretation and interpretation is everything. When we talked about memory, we discussed the way that memory is always an interpretive activity. We also discussed some thoughts that may be harmful after abuse. The following are examples of destructive thoughts reported by survivors.

One woman, who had been sexually abused by a cousin when she was six years old, decided that if she had not worn a dress and walked on a wall near this older boy, he would not have hurt her. She believed that she was immoral because she enjoyed walking on the wall and was not thinking about the fact that she was wearing a skirt and might be seen. Another woman felt that she had brought a rape upon herself because she agreed to go alone in a car with her boss to another city. The boss forced her to have sex with him. She thought that her choice to ride with him was the reason for the rape. She blamed herself and not her boss for his decision to force her. One girl believed that she had to submit to her older brother's desires because it was her duty to serve him. Once she had submitted to him, she felt she was dirty and dishonorable so it no longer mattered what happened to her. This girl began to feel powerless to stop abuse. Many women describe feeling confused when people that they truly love go past the comfortable limits of that love, and expect more intimacy than the woman wants to give. When women are raped by strangers they often believe that they were at the wrong place at the wrong time and may blame themselves for bad choices.

But it is important to remember that these thoughts and beliefs are all interpretations, stories about experiences. These interpretations do not take into account the fact that every person is responsible for their own choices. They blame the victim. But victims do not make their abusers hurt them. If a person uses someone with less power and strength for their own satisfaction, when a stronger person's needs are met at the expense of a weaker person, the stronger person is responsible for his own behavior. This can get complicated to understand. Sorting out responsibility for harm and reclaiming the strength that we have to heal is often difficult to do without talking to other trustworthy people.

It is important for survivors to remember that often one of the most damaging things about abuse is the story we tell ourselves about it. Our expectations, our social world and our self-image all contribute to the interpretations and stories we construct after abuse. But then the other side of this is true too. The stories, interpretations and meanings we give to experiences are one of the best resources we have for healing. One of the key tasks of therapy is to examine our interpretations of traumatic experiences that increase the harm, and then to construct new stories, more empowering, more encouraging stories.

Because interpretations and stories are easiest to perceive and understand when we share them with others, talking about our experiences is very important. A close and trusted friend can be a good person to hear our stories. Support groups and therapy groups are a good place to talk with other people about the thoughts and memories we have and to begin making healing stories. The luckiest of us find these people quickly and check our interpretations of difficult experiences before much time has passed. When life can quickly return to normal, and we find supportive listeners who are reassuring and help us to soothe ourselves, hurtful events do not have to become damaging. Healing can sometimes happen quickly and smoothly. This is the best situation.

If you are having trouble finding trustworthy people, or even if you have found them but want to organize your thoughts, writing can be a useful tool.

Writing and drawing give us ways to express ourselves that don't depend on having a good listener available all the time. Here are some exercises that may help you begin to make a new, more healing story for yourself about the abuse. This next activity is an expansion of the earlier exercise we called "Test Your Version of the Truth".

TRY THIS

Writing the Story Down

Find a notebook or paper that you can write on comfortably. It is best if you can make private time and a private place for yourself to write. Interruptions and interference can be a problem when you are trying to focus your attention on writing about emotional subjects. You also need to be able to keep your writing private or to safeguard the things you write after writing them. It is important that you choose when and where to share your stories. Written materials can make us feel vulnerable to other people's curiosity or judgment. If you do not have a way to safeguard your writing, consider destroying it after writing and reading it yourself. The process of writing is most important. It is less important to keep the written records after you have finished with them.

This first writing exercise can be followed up with another that we will outline later in this section. If you want to do both exercises, keep your written work long enough to complete both.

• Begin writing by answering this question: When did the abuse begin? How did the problem start?

• Write whatever comes to your mind. Don't worry about making your writing artful. The important audience for your writing is you. You need to be able to understand it. No one else should ever read it. Write freely and let the story take shape right off of your pen.

- Notice any feelings and thoughts that come to your mind as you tell this story. Make note of them and let the story follow this path.
- If you have trouble continuing, ask yourself: What happened next? Or- how do I feel about that? Or -What did I think when that happened?
- Write an account that tells the story of the abuse and the way that you think and feel about it.
- Now put your writing away for a while and take a break.
- Breathe deeply, get some exercise; talk to a friend about something completely unrelated to abuse. See if you can refocus on the present and normal life.
- If you are having trouble, go back to the "Finding Safety" (page 53) and "Facing the Pain" (page 76) sections and repeat those exercises again.

TRY THIS

Facts/ Values/ Evaluations

Allow some time to pass after you write the story down and just let it "simmer on the back burner" for a while. Often taking a step away from thinking about the story is helpful. A break can give us a chance to reflect on our thoughts, feelings and experiences without directly focusing on them. A lot of the work we do on memory and meaning making happens outside of our ordinary awareness, for instance, in dreams and daydreams. We have all had the experience of realizations about events popping up in our thoughts when we are in the middle of doing completely unrelated things. This is an indication that memory and interpretive processes are going on without our direct attention. Let this process happen, it can be helpful.

- Once again take time away from interruptions and interference. Give yourself some privacy and take out the writing you have done about your story.

- Read through your story again and look for everything in it that is a concrete fact. Facts are the kind of information that a video camera would be able to record if it recorded an event. Facts include concrete specific descriptions of events and actions that could be observable by an outside witness. Underline the facts.

- Now read the story again and find all the places where you describe an **evaluation or a judgment.** An evaluation or a judgment is a statement that includes opinions. Opinions include any statements about whether something is good or bad, judgments about meaning, value or importance. Put parenthesis ( ) around these statements or sections in your story.

- The process of interpretation began when you selected certain facts and left out others. The evaluations and judgments you are now putting in parenthesis are the next step in your interpretation. (Evaluations are an important part of building the story.) That comment is an evaluation. These evaluations and judgments are part of meaning making. Just notice them as interpretations.

- Now read the story and notice the values that are stated or that underlie the interpretations in it. **Values** are often not directly stated but are the basic beliefs that shape how we evaluate and judge events, actions and people. Values are the beliefs that create a point of view or a way of looking at the world. Some of them come from our society or culture. Some of them come from particular people around us, like our family. Some of them are things we have learned along the way.

- At the end of your story, make notes on the values that you think are revealed by the facts selected for the story and the evaluations included in it. What are the underlying values this story implicitly describes?

- Go through your entire story making these markings and then put the writing away for a time. Take another break.

101

- Now, come back and look at your marked story again and see if your point of view about the facts, values and evaluations is the same. Your interpretations may stay the same and they may change. Just notice that.

Let's look at a story to understand facts, values and evaluations better. Here is the story of Bonnie and Adam with <u>Facts</u> underlined, (Evaluations inside parenthesis), and Values described at the end.

<u>Bonnie</u> was (sexually abused) by her older brother for three years when she was between eleven and thirteen years old. She never told anyone but her younger sister. (She was afraid of how her family might react and she felt ashamed.) <u>Her sister kept the secret</u> and (Bonnie liked to think that she might have protected her sister from similar abuse by warning her about their older brother). <u>Bonnie dropped out of school part way through middle school. Her grades had been</u> (getting worse) <u>since the fifth grade when the</u> (abuse) <u>began.</u> (Eventually, school seemed too difficult, though she had done well in primary school.) <u>The</u> (abuse) <u>ended when Bonnie's brother left to do his military service. By the time her brother returned, Bonnie was married and had gone to live in her new husband's household.</u>

<u>Bonnie married Adam</u> (because her family chose him for her). (She didn't dislike him at first, but as time when on, she discovered that Adam had problems with his moods). (He was easily frustrated and irritable, and <u>after he took a job</u> under a boss who was harsh and critical), <u>Adam began to</u> (lash out) <u>verbally at Bonnie.</u> (He was angry that she didn't want to have sex with him whenever he was in the mood). (It wasn't long before <u>he began to hit her</u> when he was upset about problems at work). (Bonnie tried hard to be a good wife and make the household comfortable for Adam). <u>She cleaned and cooked and took care of their two small children.</u> (But Adam was never satisfied.) <u>The physical beatings</u> (got worse) <u>as Adam began to drink alcohol,</u> (trying to manage the dark moods that came over him more and more frequently.)

One day, Adam slapped Bonnie so hard that she fell, hit her head on a table edge and broke her jaw. When Bonnie came back to consciousness, she was looking into the tearful face of her eleven-year-old daughter. (At that moment, something snapped in her, and Bonnie decided things had to change.) *She found out about a women's support center where there were groups for women trying to recover from abuse. She began to visit the center during the day when the children were in school and Adam was away at work.*

(At the women's center Bonnie felt safe.) (She learned that (the beautiful) *openwork tablecloths her mother taught her to make could bring (a good price) from a women's cooperative sales program). (She expanded her skills to other products and began to make a little money for herself. She also learned some things about her legal rights and knew that it was not acceptable for Adam to hit her.) She began to leave the house whenever he came home drunk, taking her children with her (to a friendly) neighbor. After Adam had fallen asleep, Bonnie and the children would return home. A counselor at the women's center also taught her some body-mind skills (to help Bonnie calm herself down when she got frightened.) Bonnie taught those skills to her children as well.*

(Adam was angry that Bonnie was becoming more independent, but she didn't back down.) (More and more often) *she left the house when he began to threaten her. One day she even went to the local police station and made a complaint after he came home drunk and hit her again. Adam's brother and father spoke with Adam* (and told him that his behavior was embarrassing the family.) *They began to look for a new job for him,* (hoping that Adam would do better with a different boss). (This support from Adam's family really helped the situation; Bonnie felt stronger and Adam began to feel a little more hopeful.)

(One of the best things that happened was that) *Bonnie found out about a scholarship program. The women's center helped Bonnie's daughter to get a scholarship so that she could go to the science high school.* (The whole family was proud of her success and Bonnie knew that standing up for herself was helping her daughter to succeed too.) (Bonnie was on a path to healing, helping herself and her family.)

The evaluations and facts in stories are sometimes mixed up in the same description. It is not always possible to separate them out completely from one another. The values that a story expresses are beliefs that we can guess from looking at the evaluations. For example, let's look at just the last two sentences. (*The whole family was proud of her success and Bonnie knew that standing up for herself was helping her daughter to succeed too. Bonnie was on a path to healing, helping herself and her family.*) These statements imply a number of values.

For instance, the family feels included and good about the success of one of their family members. This shows valuing of family connectedness, and approval for accomplishment. This family values education. A mother can feel a sense of accomplishment in the achievements of her children; this is a belief. Bonnie standing up for herself is a good thing; this is a judgment. Healing includes not only helping ourselves but also helping others to feel stronger and be more accomplished. These are just a few of the values that we can understand from reading this pair of sentences. Values and beliefs are an important part of the structure of meaning that can be found under everything we think, feel and do.

Reframing Destructive Thoughts

So what is the point of picking out the Facts, Values and Evaluations in a story? First and foremost the point is to become more aware of which parts of our thoughts and feelings are based upon facts, which parts are based on feelings and evaluations, and which parts of the story are ways of stating our values and beliefs. When we do an exercise like this, we begin to become more aware of our own interpretations of events. It is often easier to perceive the way someone else is judging and valuing than it is for us to reflect on our thinking about ourselves. Interpretations are sometimes helpful to us; sometimes they are hurtful. It is difficult to change hurtful thoughts if we aren't aware that they are interpretations. We cannot consider changing beliefs that we don't really know about. This exercise can help you to reconsider beliefs that may be hurting you and reexamine judgments and interpretations that may be giving you problems.

The process of changing our interpretation of an event is called reframing it. When we change the thoughts around an experience, we are reframing our experience. For example in the story of Bonnie and Adam, Bonnie begins with a belief that she needs to: (*be a good wife and make the household comfortable for Adam.*) She believes that she needs to tolerate his violent behavior in order to be a "good wife". It is not until she is badly injured and sees the fear in the eyes of her eleven year old daughter -an age when Bonnie was abused by her own brother- that Bonnie decides not to "be good" in the way that she has tried to be in the past.

She makes a new choice and looks for support so that she can be less dependent on her husband and take care of her family differently. She finds the women's center and starts to do things that let her take care of herself and her family differently. She begins to see her ability to make a little bit of money and her choice to take the children and leave the house when Adam is drunk as a different way of being a good mother and wife. She is acting on a different value or belief; this belief says that a good mother and wife protects her children from the violent behavior of their father. A good mother does not make herself available for abuse from her husband, she stands up to him, saying no. Bonnie's version of a strong family is supported by Adam's father and brother, a women's center and friendly neighbors.

Hiding Adam's abusive behavior is no longer framed in Bonnie's mind and actions as part of being a good wife. Instead, she has framed getting help and confronting the abuse as strengthening her family.

Let's look at another example of reframing. In the list of destructive thoughts we described in the section "Interpreting Again" a woman had decided that she was an immoral six year old because she enjoyed walking on a wall in a skirt and her older cousin had seen her and then sexually abused her. She framed her enjoyment of walking on a wall and the fact that her cousin noticed her and paid attention to her as immoral.

However, this is very adult thinking about a six-year-old mind. Six year olds frequently enjoy physical activity for the simple pleasure of the body skills they are developing. The feeling of physical competence and the pleasure of having another person notice the child and her new skill is a completely natural and a very common way for a six year old to think and to feel. Generally speaking, six year olds love attention but do not frame it in terms of their sexual attractiveness or a desire to evoke sexual feelings in other people. Those are motivations that are characteristic of people after puberty or in adulthood.

When adults say that they think a child is trying to attract them sexually, they are almost always projecting their own desires onto the mind of the child. It is true that a child can be trained by adults to sexualize their thoughts and feelings. Attention is very important to everyone, and if the attention that a child can get from others is mostly related to their sexual behavior or appearance, a child can learn to behave in sexually pleasing ways. But this is a distortion of children's natural desire to be competent, pleasing and valued. The adult is the person who has put a sexual, moral interpretation onto the child's behavior, not the child.

Once again the issue of power has been obscured in the story of the immoral six-year-old girl. In fact, her father raised her making interpretations of all her behavior in terms of her sexuality as a girl. He demanded that her dress, movements, and friendships conform to strict rules that he defined as moral, honorable behavior. Her father is the person who put a sexual interpretation onto her behavior, and the girl learned that belief. A girl does not have as much power to define her own behavior and values as her parents. But this interpretation of her natural, childish behavior is harmful to the girl and then later to the woman.

After her cousin took advantage of her youth and vulnerability, she decided that since she was immoral anyway, it didn't matter who she allowed to touch or use her. She did not feel worthy of good friends and kind treatment. Her life and relationships unfolded in tragic ways as a result of these beliefs.

Reframing this belief involves understanding her six-year-old behavior in more developmentally informed ways. With accurate information about the way six year olds tend to think and behave, this woman can recognize that her cousin was out of line. He was making the "immoral" choice. He was at fault for this exploitative choice and he should be held responsible for hurting her. The cousin needed to be held accountable and re-trained about how to act respectfully toward other people. This is the process of reframing, and it includes holding abusive people accountable.

In both the cases we have discussed, reframing of the experience shifted the way that these women were blaming themselves for the bad things that had happened to them. Once the responsibility for the problem was placed where it actually belongs, on the person perpetrating the abuse, these women could use their awareness to consider new choices for themselves. This is an important part of the process of healing.

5. Moving On

Recovery, Confidence and Empowerment

For many survivors, recovery and healing has a lot to do with using their new interpretations, their new stories to set aside old feelings of self-blame. Negative self-images are questioned and reframed to discover new confidence.

Self-confidence is a sense of trust and hope that things can come out well for you. Before recovery, survivors of sexual abuse often find it very difficult to feel confident. But this kind of hope and trust is damaged by abuse and then restored by recovery. In order to put abuse experiences behind us, to make abuse part of our past and no longer an obstacle in our present or future, we must restore confidence and hope. The restoration of confidence and the development of skills to take care of ourselves is the basis of empowerment.

Recovery then should be empowering. Moving on from abuse is returning to a sense of strength, health and wholeness. Holding onto or feeling stuck with the identity of having been a victim of sexual abuse is not full recovery. Labeling others or ourselves as victims, seeing our life experiences always in terms of the results of abuse is not empowerment. A person who has healed can acknowledge that sexual abuse is a part of their history; healing will not erase the effects of abuse, we may carry scars. But a person who has healed no longer feels defined or shaped primarily by that event.

This can be tricky, because some people say that their abuse was not important. There are many people who say that they do not believe that the abuse experience harmed them. "I have dealt with that." "I don't worry about that anymore." "That was a long time ago and it doesn't affect me now." Survivors frequently make this sort of comment. Sometimes it is true;

the abuse is no longer an issue affecting the person's life and relationships. But sometimes the effects are present as depression, anxiety, a poor self-image, poor relationships or some of the other signs we discussed in the first section of this guide. When a person thinks they have dealt with the abuse and put it behind them, but they continue to have symptoms and signs of emotional, psychological and relational problems, it is worth considering whether the healing has really been completed.

Goal Setting and Recovery

Each woman best defines recovery in her own terms. Because we all have somewhat different values, standards and hopes for ourselves, it is best to decide what a good life means for yourself. The following exercises are intended to help you develop and clarify your values, hopes and goals for yourself.

TRY THIS

Where Will You Be When You Have Recovered?

Many people find it a little easier to start thinking about goals with a drawing or a picture, something that doesn't depend on words.

- Find paper, and if you can, color crayons, pens or pencils so that you can use different colors. Some people enjoy cutting pictures out of magazines and pasting them onto paper as a way of making this image.
- Whatever works best for you, create an image of where you will be, who and how you will be, when you have recovered. Be as rich and complete in this image as you can. Who are you when you are at your best, and when you feel whole, healthy and strong? What kind of a place will you be in? Where will you be living? What will you be doing? Who will be there with you? Who will not be there?

- Use colors, and don't worry about the artistic quality of your picture. This is not a work of art; this is an image to let your imagination speak to you. Play with it and take your time.
- After you are finished with this image, set it beside you and make a list of the goals that it seems to show.
- Note: What are you doing? Who have you become? What are the people, places and things around you? Are these your goals? Please take the image you have created and use it as a starting point for defining your own goals. For example does the image show you doing some kind of work? Are you alone or with others? Who is with you? How are you relating to the people who are there with you? What kind of a location or home are you in? And so on.
- Take your time with this part of the exercise. This task of turning the image into a list may take a few days, or even longer.
- It can be especially fun and illuminating to do this exercise with other women around you. A group of trusted friends can often do this exercise together, each working on their own image and personal goals. The images that result from doing this project in a group are often more fun, richer and more complete than if we work alone. If you can find friends to do this activity with you, go ahead.
- A person does not have to have experienced abuse or be trying to solve a major life problem to benefit from this activity. Any woman can do this along with you. Have fun and play with it!

TRY THIS

What Is the Road to Your New Life?

- Now you can make a second picture if you like. This picture can go beside the picture of you after your recovery, but this is the picture of how you get there. What is the road, the path, or the direction that you take to get to your recovered self?
- Again, use colors, pictures clipped from magazines, anything that helps you to imagine the way that you will be going toward your goals.
- It may not be clear how to get all the way from where you are to those goals. Most of us do not know all the steps we have to take on the way to our goals until we are travelling on the path. But you may have some ideas. What is the landscape that you will go through? What are the events, the markers, the turning points and choices that you are likely to come upon as you travel from where you are now to where you want to be? Let your imagination roam.
- Even if you cannot answer all your own questions now, maybe you will discover that you do know a few things. This picture should help you learn about what may be involved in getting from where you are now to where you want to be.
- Take your time and do this exercise with friends if that is helpful.

TRY THIS

First Steps

This is the final exercise in this set of three related activities:

- Now you have an image of where you want to go, who you want to be, and you have some ideas about how to go there and what you might meet along the way.

- Next, it is time to decide what the first steps on this journey might be. If you want to go to the place you have described, what are the first things that you can do today, tomorrow, and this week to begin to follow that path?
- Make a list divided into two columns. In the first column write down a task, something you can do. Set yourself some clear tasks to accomplish.
- In the second column, beside each task, write down a realistic time period in which to do it.
- For instance, if you need to get help for your health, legal support or social services for yourself or your family, what are the first steps toward those things? Who can you talk to? Who can you call? Where can you go to visit with the right people? Think about things that can be done right away.
- Write these tasks down in the first column and the time the task should be complete in the second. These are your first steps. For example:

Task	Date Finished
Talk to my friend about doing some of the activities in this book together	Today
Find a notebook to use for activities	Today
Call the local government authority to ask if there is a women's counseling center nearby	Tomorrow

Do you have a trusted friend or person who can help you to do these things? At the very least, it may be a good idea to have someone else know that you want to take these steps and that you are planning to help yourself in these ways. Maybe it would be good to have this trusted friend go along with you to find services. Maybe your friend can take care of your children while you go, so that you do not have to watch them while you are dealing with a bureaucratic task. Maybe it would just help to have someone know that you want to do this, so that they can encourage you and tell you that they believe you can do it too. This is part of what being a good support person is.

A trustworthy friend will respect your goals and help you to reach them. Sometimes your friend may have suggestions for practical, realistic steps to take toward your goal. But a friend who does not respect your goals, who does not respect your wishes for yourself is not a respectful, trustworthy friend. Listen to advice, but test it against your own ideas too. With other people's support, begin to take the steps that lead you toward your own idea of recovery. You are already on the journey to recovery. Keep going. Don't give up. Believe in yourself and find the right support.

Expecting Miracles But Not Magic

Because survivors' hope and faith in the future has often been damaged, it can be difficult to believe that good things will happen again after abuse. But after working many years with many women recovering from sexual abuse, there is absolutely no doubt that women can recover fully. It is possible for survivors to become even stronger and more powerful people than they were before the abuse. In recent years, people working with trauma survivors have begun to talk more and more about post-traumatic growth and resilience. There is nothing good about trauma and we do not mean to praise abuse. However, it is clear that some people recover very fully and become especially strong and confident. You can be one of the people who turn traumatic experiences into an opportunity for growth and greater wisdom.

Many women who undergo treatment for serious emotional and relationship consequences after abuse use the hope they gain from therapy to go back to school or improve their work situations. Increased confidence translating into more education and better employment opportunities are among the most common outcomes of therapy for sexual abuse survivors. Another very common outcome of trauma treatment for survivors of sexual abuse is improved relationships with family members. Many survivors find new ways to relate to important family members and improve their communication skills in the course of therapy. Identifying new goals and more sustainable ideas about how to have healthy relationships and families are among the primary objectives of healing from sexual abuse.

The important thing to note here is that the hopeless, helpless feelings that so many abuse and trauma survivors feel, are temporary. With the right support and help, a person can put abuse behind them. Too often people who have experienced abuse want to forget about it and push away the pain, hoping that the whole thing will pass away. There are times when this strategy does indeed work. There are times however when the "forget about it and it will go away" strategy does not work at all. Turning away and acting as if the abuse never happened is not necessary. If turning away, getting on with ordinary life and taking good care of yourself with the help of family and friends is not working well enough, pay attention. If you discover that you are having the kinds of symptoms discussed in the first section of this guide and there is a history of sexual abuse in your life, you have choices. With the right support you can face the pain and not only put the experience behind you, but also learn useful and strengthening lessons from it. It may seem impossible, but in fact, the miracle of reclaiming an excellent life is very possible. Every person has the capacity to recover, with support.

Many times when a sexual abuse survivor who has been seriously affected considers the possibility of healing, feeling really good and whole again seems impossible. A sense that she is helpless or that the situation is hopeless is in fact one of the psychological effects of abuse that begins when a person is quite young. These feelings can also last a very long time. But, helplessness and hopelessness are not the truth. Survivors are not helpless and the situation is not hopeless. On the other hand, sometimes healing does seem like a miracle. Sometimes we feel as if the results are hard to imagine, even miraculous. You may find that completely unexpected or un-predictable things will occur. Having seen the miracle of healing over and over again, those of us who work with abuse survivors know it is not magic. Real effort and skillful, careful work is necessary, but the results are well worth the effort. Don't wait to have faith in miracles, try putting one foot in front of the other and you will discover that your journey has begun.

There are also times when a survivor feels so helpless or hopeless, she believes someone else, a hero or a magician, needs to come along and save her. In fact, the magic we are looking for is inside of us. The cure is in your hands. There is no hero who can deliver you from the dragon of this pain, only yourself. In the process of becoming and acting as your own hero, you will be amazed by what you can do. But the magic is something you will see afterwards. Looking for heroes, saviors, or magical cures is a sure way to disappointment, and in fact often leads to more harm. In the next section we will talk more about the difference between a heroic rescuer and a true friend and helper. But right now please be assured: the hero you seek is you; the magic is inside of you. It is not that you have to do everything alone. No one recovers completely alone. But learning to find, and trust, and take appropriate support from true friends is what the journey of recovery from sexual abuse is all about. We hope this guide can help you to find the miracle of recovery that you seek.

Here are a few examples of changes that women have made after facing and healing from sexual abuse.

• One woman in a trauma therapy group decided that she and her hus-band could reconcile, if they agreed to certain ground rules and committed to no violence and some positive trust building behaviors with one another.

Six months later, after they followed the plan together, she was still married and feeling much better about her relationship with her husband.

• One woman in a trauma treatment group believed that she was physically deformed and ugly and so could not find the courage to have any relationship with a man. At the end of the group, she had begun to have friendly meetings with a man she liked. Within a year they married and another year later she let her old therapists know that she was pregnant.

• One woman had been unhappily married for many years to a man she regretted letting her family persuade her to marry. She decided finally to divorce.

• One woman had never been able to complete an academic degree that she had been working on for several years, making little progress. She finally found the strength to complete the work and get her degree.

• One woman realized that she had the skills to do much more responsible work, applied for a managerial position in her company and won it.

• One woman, who had withdrawn from many activities and friendships after a rape, discovered new courage after treatment. She decided to return to work and began to plan to found a new business along with some friends of hers. Her strength and energy returned and she felt she was a much better mother after recovery than she had been before the rape.

Some day you will turn around and think, 'It is over. I am a tree growing in a forest among other trees. I was affected by a rock that lay in my path. An extra weight or burden was placed in my way. But after having pushed up against that obstacle, I finally found a way to grow around it. If I look closely, I can still see the way that stone affected my growth, the rock may still be lying there. But now, I have grown around and past that stone. I am not held down or harmed by it any more. In fact, the process of growing around it taught me useful things. Now I have moved on. I am free of the weight of the stone, I have healed and I am whole.'

The day will come when your life is no longer seriously affected by your past experiences of abuse. We hope this guide and the true friends you will find to help you along your way will provide valuable support for your healing. We also hope that you will continue to seek out whatever you need until you are satisfied with your own recovery.

There will be some people who need to find expert psychological help like individual or group psychotherapy to help them heal from their abuse experiences. There is not enough space in this handbook to describe the details of psychotherapy. But many people find that dealing with some of the most intense emotional and body-mind symptoms is made less difficult by working with a well-trained mental health professional. If you think your emotions or physical symptoms are more than you can handle alone or with friends and you have access to well-trained mental health therapists, therapy has been shown to be very effective. Both individual and group therapy have shown excellent results for many abuse survivors. There is evidence that group therapy with other survivors of sexual abuse is particularly effective. We hope you can find this kind of support if you need it.

PART III

Being a True Friend
(and why it isn't easy)

1. Why True Friends Are So Important

This section of our guide is written for the people who care about and want to support women who have been sexually abused. Some true friends are family members, some of you are good friends, some of you are people who voluntarily or professionally serve women who have been abused. All of you are necessary for her full recovery process. Abuse occurs in human relationships and the process of recovery from abuse also depends upon healthy relationships. Healthy relationships are based upon offering sincere care that understands its own limits. Healthy, empowering help both respects a survivor's strengths and understands her needs.

Once again we emphasize that this book is written as a guide for adults and people who want to help adults. This book is not written in the correct style for child survivors to read. People helping children will also need additional information.

Certain differences between adults and children are quite clear. Children are not in a position to make some important decisions for themselves and do not have enough knowledge or experience to protect and care for themselves independently as adults do. The adults who are responsible for children must help guide their choices more directly than those helping adult survivors. Important differences make the process of healing slightly different when survivors are still children.

By this we do not mean that child survivors cannot be involved in making choices and decisions about their lives. On the contrary, it is often very good to give children information and involve them in discussions about decisions that will have a major impact on their lives. Those discussions and the level of a child's involvement in decisions about healing depend on the child's age and stage of development. We are not going to discuss child development in great detail here. A much more thorough consideration of developmental stages and ability to understand opportunities and consequences is necessary when working specifically with children. We hope that such a guide will also be written some day. But in this guide we are focusing on healing for survivors who are adults.

When a woman's friends are true friends, they want to see that the woman emerges stronger and more confident, better able to make healthy choices and live more fully than immediately after abuse. Unfortunately, there are people who confuse being a friend with being a rescuer. Sometimes a person wants to be a friend and be helpful but they are confused about the role that they should play. This is especially tricky because many people who have been abused are also hoping for a hero or a magician to come along and make everything better. It is easy to get confused about what kind of help is real help.

A true friend is not going to "save" or "rescue" a survivor. They will protect, support, encourage, and sometimes even guide and advise the survivor. But when someone steps in and tries to take over, when another person decides that they know best what is right for an adult survivor, that person adds to the problem. If we behave as if a survivor should simply accept protection and do as they are told, we are not acting like a true friend.

But many of us are not sure what to say and what not to say. We are unclear about how to be helpful and what actions may be harmful. If we are close to someone who has experienced abuse we may also feel confused or disturbed by changes we observe in them. Or if the abuse happened long before we met the person, we may find some of their behaviors strange or confusing because these behaviors do not fit with the situation in the present. It is possible to do additional harm if we try to help a survivor inappropriately. This section will give you guidance and information so that you can be as effective and empowering as possible when offering support to survivors of sexual abuse.

The Rescue Triangle

In the 1960's a man named Karpman developed a model of interaction that is helpful for understanding some of the pitfalls of trying to rescue people in situations of abuse. I will describe a modified version of his model. Understanding the roles of the people involved may help to illustrate why too often efforts to rescue someone who has been harmed by abuse don't turn out the way we hope. In fact, it is common to find that after we have tried to help someone dealing with abuse, they may at first seem grateful but then later become angry with us. Another common experience for people who try to help is to find that our suggestions and advice are not taken or are accepted at first but then later ignored or rejected. Even when our intentions are very good and our desire to help is real, we may be seen as hurtful or bullying. Let's look at how this happens.

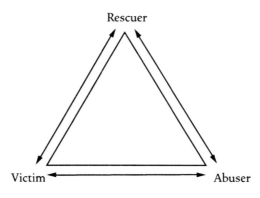

- Rescue Triangle Diagram -

In situations of abuse there are at least three distinct roles, that of the Victim, the Abuser and the Rescuer. On the surface these roles and the types of actions associated with them seem obvious. A Victim is a person who has been hurt. An Abuser is a person who hurts others through misuse of power and control. A Rescuer is a person who tries to help the Victim so that they can be saved from the harm of the Abuser.

But the problem is that the Victim may become stuck in seeing herself as a weak and powerless person who needs a Rescuer to save her from Abusers. She may believe that the job of the Rescuer is simply to save her. She may believe that she does not have the power to do anything but passively accept the efforts of the Rescuer to save her. She may believe that she has been hurt forever by the misuse of power and control by the Abuser. As long as the Victim views the situation through the lens that she is powerless, there is a risk that any powerful Rescuer may begin to look like an Abuser to her too. If a Rescuer says things that the Victim does not want to hear, or tries to do things that the Victim does not want done, then she may turn and begin to view her Rescuer as a new Abuser. This can be very confusing for a well intentioned Rescuer who is only trying to help.

The basic problem is that a Rescuer will always be in danger of seeming to become an Abuser unless the Victim understands that she too can make choices and exercise strength. If a Victim is stuck in a weak position, she can never get better or stronger and she will stay under the power and control of other people.

When a Victim begins to find some ways that she too can be strong and act with choice, she can step out of the Victim role and see her own strength. If she can be strong too, she is no longer just a victim. Every person wants to have some power and control in her own life, no matter how comforting it may be at times to let other people take responsibility for us.

Rescuers may also be surprised sometimes to find that they have begun to feel like a victim of the Victim. After trying to help or giving advice, a Rescuer can be very confused by an angry or a rejecting response from a Victim. A Victim may at first accept help and then turn around and accuse a Rescuer of hurting or bullying her. The well meaning Rescuer may become angry and simply see the Victim as ungrateful or even stupid for not taking the Rescuer's advice.

We all have had the experience of taking responsibility and then later discovering that we are blamed because something has gone wrong. The best way to avoid this is to share responsibility, to avoid taking more than our share. When we expect others to have good ideas and welcome shared contributions toward a solution, we are more likely to avoid this problem.

The third corner of the triangle can also move; the Abuser often complains that he is in fact a Victim. Many Abusers say that they did what they did because the Victim made them do it, or somehow provoked the attack. Abusers also often argue that in fact they are a Rescuer, not an Abuser. They frequently believe that they are acting in the best interests or satisfying the wishes of the Victim. Abusers almost never perceive themselves as abusive, they almost always believe they are misunderstood or unappreciated. They usually do not understand their own misuse of power and control.

In other words then, each of the roles, each of the positions on the three corners of the triangle may move. Each person, Victim, Rescuer and Abuser may see themselves, or want to be seen, differently than others see them. No role is actually fixed. Victims and Rescuers can be very attached to seeing themselves in those roles. But in fact these roles, like so much else, are a matter of interpretation. People tend to believe that their good intentions determine their role. They may have trouble accepting that, in spite of their intentions, they play out different roles in other people's interpretations. Abuser is the one role that nobody wants, and Abusers almost always describe themselves as being in one of the other two positions. Here are some examples of these changing role interpretations.

****

Sara grew up in a very traditional, conservative family. The rules were strict, her parents wanted to protect her from the dangers of society. There were times when Sara felt smothered and over-controlled by her family, sometimes she even felt like a victim of their control. But she knew their intentions for her were good. Sara was relieved when she was 19 and her parents chose a husband for her. Rami was the son of neighbors, another good, traditional family. Sara hoped that this marriage would be a way for her to gain some breathing room after her very restrictive family life. Rami seemed capable and strong. Perhaps he could be a rescuer, get her out and give her more choices.

Things went pretty well for a while. Rami was working and Sara got pregnant and everything seemed to be going according to plan. Sara felt better, more like her life was her own. But then Rami lost his job. When their income dried up and Rami had to ask for help from his family, he became frustrated and wanted to exercise more control over Sara. He no longer trusted her with any of the family money. He wanted to do all the family shopping and gave her no voice in family decisions. Sara felt crushed and controlled again. She began to resent Rami's control.

When their baby was born, Sara was focused on being a good mother. Rami felt very responsible for the family and was worried about how he would support them without a job. He began to pressure Sara for sex more frequently, just when she felt less interested in having sex with him. With a new baby and her own body still recovering from the birth, Sara was not eager for sex, but Rami seemed to want it even more. Sara was uncomfortable but accepted that she should satisfy Rami. He got angry that she was so uninterested; it hurt his pride. One day Sara was especially tired and Rami got especially upset and forceful. He roughly forced Sara to have sex, ignoring her cries of pain and dismay. He wanted to show her that as her husband, she owed him sex when he wanted it. Sara felt abused and hurt. She was angry and resentful of

Rami's control and misuse of his greater physical strength. Her desire for sex with him dropped even further.

Of course in reality this story would not end here. Both Sara and Rami may look for rescue from other family members or from other friends. Both of them feel like victims, both feel abused or mistreated by the other. The cycle of frustration, victimization, misuse of power and control and a desire to be rescued by someone else are likely to escalate. Rami may not see the superior power his physical strength and male social position give him, but they are real.

Here is a different example especially relevant to people that help women fleeing family violence.

Hannah had been married for ten years to Ali and the marriage was problematic from the first. Hannah's family married her off at sixteen in a religious ceremony, though her official marriage was not until she was of legal age at 18. Hannah had completed fifth grade and her family wanted to be sure she married before she got into any trouble. Hannah had three children during the first ten years of her marriage, two girls, now 8 and 7, and then a boy, now 5 years old. Ali had a quick temper and had the bad habit of hitting Hannah when he was angry. Hannah knew that if Ali was ever dissatisfied with anything in the household, if the soup was too salty, if the salon was not tidy enough, if one of the children misbehaved, he would hit her for punishment. Once he broke her arm, and she had permanent ringing in her left ear from a time he banged her head against a wall.

Hannah resisted the beatings after a while. This treatment seemed unjust to her. She argued with Ali at times, but the beatings just became worse. Eventually, Ali began to hit their two daughters when something at home or at school displeased him. He complained to Hannah that the girls dressed like whores and tore up the oldest daughter's favorite blouse. He was constantly checking up on the girls' activity outside the household and frequently hit them when they did things he didn't approve of. Hannah could no longer tolerate the violence when it began to affect her daughters as well. What she didn't know that Ali was also going to the girls' bedroom at night and touching them on their genitals for his own pleasure. The girls were too afraid of him to say anything about it to Hannah. She heard about a shelter house in a big city nearby, took her children with her and fled to that city asking for help.

Hannah was accepted with her children into the shelter house. Immediately, the shelter house staff encouraged her to consider her choices and began to offer her opportunities for unskilled work. Hannah was relieved to be away from all the beatings and was glad her children were safe. The children were relieved to be away from their father but still too afraid to talk about all the abuse. But as Hannah began to consider what her life would be like if she divorced Ali and had to live on her own, she began to feel afraid again. She hated being beaten, but the kind of work she could get, cleaning other people's houses, perhaps making tea in an office, always working long hours at very low pay, did not look attractive either. She asked the shelter house staff to help her find better jobs, but none could be found for someone with her low level of education. Hannah began to feel trapped and angry. She began to argue with the shelter house staff and complain about the limited help they could offer. Hannah wanted a better life and this new life was not as good as what she had been hoping for. She began to consider going back to Ali.

The shelter house staff warned her that if she went back, she should be prepared that Ali might continue to hit her and the girls. Hannah knew this was true but she hoped that maybe Ali had learned a lesson and would behave better now. After about four weeks in the shelter house, Hannah returned to Ali, hoping for the best. The shelter house staff was worried that she was putting her children in danger but they had to accept her choice. Six months later Hannah came back, asking for shelter again. This time Ali had beaten the oldest daughter very badly one night when she returned home late after being at a friend's house. The girl had required stitches in her head and was bleeding from one kidney after blows to her back. The cycle of family violence went on.

The shelter house staff had tried to rescue Hannah, an obvious victim. And Hannah was not able to protect her children, who were also victims. The shelter house staff was frustrated when she returned to Ali, who was clearly abusive. But no one was in a position to provide the kind of rescue from abuse that Hannah wished for. The children were caught up in the problem too. Some of what they were suffering wasn't even out in the open. As long as Ali was not held accountable for his violent and abusive behavior, and as long as Hannah could not get more education or job skills training, she was trapped in a vicious cycle - stuck being a victim. The children too were trapped as victims.

A really good and lasting solution can be difficult to find. Lasting solutions to family violence depend upon a combination of accountability for abusers, protection and empowerment for victims and prevention through making family violence unacceptable in society. This combination of strategies shifts all three roles and has the best likelihood of making a difference that breaks the cycle of violence. This guide is focused on methods for empowering victims, helping them transform into survivors, along with preventing future violence by showing the ways that everyone in society has a stake in reducing sexual abuse.

2. Secondary Trauma

People who work to support survivors and prevent future abuse also face another significant challenge called secondary trauma. In addition to understanding the dynamics of interactions between people and the roles that they tend to play, helpers also have to understand the way that trauma can be made worse in the process of trying to help. Secondary trauma is an additional layer of hurt that can affect either the survivor of abuse or people who are trying to help her, sometimes both. People working with survivors of all kinds of trauma have discovered that there are significant hazards when helping people trying to recover from abuse. While we wish the process of recovery were simple, it turns out that it is not. Not all help is actually helpful. Let's look first at some of the risks to the survivor from well intentioned but unskilled help.

Risks to the Survivor

Most people like the feeling of being able to help others. It makes us feel better and stronger to be able to do good things for others. Generosity and kindness often feel very good and can be rewarding for the giver. Unfortunately, there are times when the kind of help we want to give or the type of help we believe is needed is not actually the help that the survivor needs most. Some help is not very helpful.

For instance, sometimes help gives an abused person the message that they cannot recover without other people taking over, protecting and directing their lives. The type of help that increases psychologically dangerous feelings of helplessness and powerlessness is not helpful. Short term improvement of a dangerous situation begins with protection. There is a stage when the immediate need of a survivor is simply to be kept away from harm. This is fine for a while, but this is just a first stage in recovery.

The next stage of recovery requires helping a woman to see the ways that she can exercise strength and choice. When a woman first leaves an abusive situation, she needs to rest in a safe place and calm down enough to assess her own needs and desires. She usually has been unable to focus on what she needs for herself up until the time she makes her way to a more sheltered, safe place. But from the safety of a refuge she needs support and encouragement to take the next steps into a stronger, healthier life. Recovery should be a process that unfolds in stages. Getting stuck in the first stage of protection, simply sheltering a woman away from harm, eventually may deepen her sense of powerlessness and hopelessness. This reinforcement of dependency and helplessness is one type of secondary trauma for survivors.

Another form of secondary trauma for survivors is pushing them to talk about the abuse and face the harm they experienced in ways that only increase their fear and hyper-sensitivity. Society is often silent and in turn silence is often expected of survivors of abuse. This begins as self-protection but eventually becomes damaging. Talking about the ugly experiences of sexual abuse is painful for everyone. The degree of social silence and avoidance of trauma awareness and memory in many societies is far too great. We do not advocate avoiding talk about trauma. However, there is an opposing point of view that holds that silence is never desirable. This point of view believes that if we can get people to talk about their abuse experiences, exposure itself is good. If we can all just express our feelings and tell our stories, everything will be all right. Unfortunately, the situation is not that simple.

The self protective instinct to avoid trauma, and to ignore thoughts and feelings associated with it, is sensible in the beginning. Talking about and facing the feelings and memories associated with traumatic experience is very intense. As we discussed in the earlier sections of this book, setting up the right conditions for inner and outer safety before facing overwhelming thoughts and feelings is extremely important. People trying to help will sometimes decide that the painful truth must be faced before a survivor has gained enough outward safety or learned enough about inner safety. When a survivor of abuse is pushed too early or unprepared into dealing with traumatic memories and feelings, their fear, helplessness, hopelessness and pain can be increased rather than relieved. Post-trauma symptoms may increase dramatically. This is also a form of secondary trauma.

Helpers often need to be very patient and calm, building the strength of their relationship with the survivor and increasing the sense of interpersonal safety and trust. Creating safety is not the same for every person and while the process of recovery will always involve some risk, it is important not to force recovery. It is true that a few people may never feel strong enough to face their fears, but most people become braver and more ready to face frightening things when they are skillfully supported and encouraged. Above all, good friends and helpers should expect that the process of recovery will take time and the best way to move forward is gently and with trust, not with force. Remember that abuse is a misuse of power and force; help is not helpful when it is forced.

People who have been sexually abused often tell stories of going to friends or professionals for help who say things that increase the shame and hurt, or who try to force a solution. Well-meaning family members may try to protect but end up blaming the victim. People who should be protecting may refuse to pay attention or overreact with protection that feels more like holding the survivor in jail. Counselors may ignore the requests of a survivor and give her the services they want her to accept rather than the services she believes she really needs. Mental health professionals without enough knowledge and training in the area of abuse may do additional damage with bad advice or harmful interpretations. And these are the people who mean well. There are also plenty of people in society who have no sympathy for survivors and intentionally do them harm. Too often one harmful experience can lead a survivor into others.

The reasons survivors tend to keep silent are many. This type of secondary trauma, or the ways that seeking help for abuse can lead survivors to additional hurt is a real concern. There are times when it is better to do nothing at all rather than to offer a partial solution or a bit of help that in the end actually weakens survivors' own strategies for taking care of themselves. We can see this in the way that family violence tends to increase when families move away from their accustomed homes. One of the highest levels of family violence has been reported in newly urbanized or displaced immigrant and refugee families.

These families are living in circumstances that isolate them from the family ties and social supports that used to help provide safety and protection for them. Traditional societies often have mechanisms in place that encourage people to behave well toward one another and that include forms of accountability for most people. Disrupted families and dislocated families naturally are under stress and strain. The evidence worldwide shows that refugee and immigrant families suffer some of the highest rates of family violence.

Risks to the Helper

Another kind of secondary trauma is a very real concern for people who work voluntarily or professionally with survivors of trauma. This can also be a hazard for friends and family of survivors, but people who work intensively or over a long period of time with survivors of abuse are at great risk for this type of secondary trauma (sometimes called vicarious trauma). For reasons related to the way that our brains, nervous systems and emotions work, people who work with trauma survivors may begin to experience symptoms that are similar to trauma affects. Some of the effects of trauma seem to be subtly transmitted to people who are not directly involved but who work closely with trauma survivors.

People who work with survivors of trauma and who are not taking enough care to protect themselves from this type of secondary trauma report high levels of stress. They also report depression, anxiety, irritability, and very often a pattern of symptoms that is called "burn out". Burn out is a characteristic pattern of fatigue, decrease in interest and enjoyment from accustomed pleasures, decreased sensitivity toward the suffering of others, and an overall increase in cynicism and negative attitudes.

One of the trickiest things about secondary trauma affects on helpers is that they are often difficult for the affected helper to notice. Because secondary trauma tends to be cumulative, in other words, because it tends to build up over time. After working with many people struggling with traumatic experiences, symptoms of burn out can develop gradually without us noticing them.

It is common for those who work with traumatized people to begin working with great enthusiasm and energy and then over time to gradually become disillusioned, disappointed and finally quit or become insensitive. Many people begin working with an idealistic desire to help, then exhaust themselves, become discouraged and leave to find easier work. It is important not to devote one's life solely to working as a helper. The people who want to be able to do this kind of work effectively for a long time must learn to take good care of themselves. Everyone gains from the knowledge of highly experienced helpers. Taking good care of the helper is taking good care of everyone they care for too.

Being a true good friend to sexual abuse survivors means taking good care of one's self too. First, a caregiver must notice their own signs of fatigue, decreasing sensitivity to others and increasing emotional discomfort. Next, they must have a good list of skills to use to take care of themself. Exercise, eating a healthy diet, getting plenty of rest and sleep, spending time with positive friends and having fun, satisfying hobbies, enjoyable activities, sports, music, art, dance ... the list goes on and on.

If you work professionally or as a volunteer in an organization that serves trauma survivors you will need professional supervision for support. The important thing is to know which activities are best for you, how to take good care of yourself, and then to do these things. It is easy to neglect these things when other people's needs seem urgent. But neglecting care for yourself will only decrease your ability to care for others over the long run.

3. Boundaries - What Are They?

One of the things people who want to help others must learn is to have good boundaries. But what does that mean? There are several parts to having good boundaries: 1) know your limits, 2) keep your own emotional balance, 3) don't let someone else's crisis become yours, 4) pay close attention to your own needs even when you are attending to others. Let's look at these ways of thinking about boundaries one by one.

1. Know Your Limits.

Everyone has limits. There are limits to every person's knowledge, no matter how expert. There are limits to every person's energy, no matter how strong. There are limits to everyone's emotional capacity, no matter how big hearted. Each of these types of limits are something we need to know about ourselves so that when we are coming to the limits of our knowledge, energy or emotional strength, we can stop before we go too far. Knowing our limits provides protection both for ourselves and for the people we want to help.

For instance, in the case of knowledge, common sense can tell us a lot about what a survivor of sexual abuse needs, but there are things that we may not understand without special training. A doctor may need to check the condition of the survivor's body and take care of medical problems. A lawyer understands the laws and how to help her protect her legal rights. A social worker may be necessary to help her access the social services she needs. Friends certainly offer important psychological support, but there are times when the situation will become too serious or complicated for friends to manage alone. In those cases, it may be necessary for a person trained in the psychology of trauma to be involved. Even psychologists may find that they need additional information or skills to work effectively with trauma.

No one should be afraid to admit that there are parts of a sexual abuse survivor's needs that they cannot fulfill alone. Our limits are to be expected and accepted. When we reach our limits, we should cooperate with others to find the knowledge and skills our friend needs. We will talk more in the next section about specific health, legal and social service needs that abuse survivors may have.

We all have limits to our energy as well. The needs of a person who has been traumatized can be very great indeed. They may be afraid of being alone. They may have complicated reactions that require lots of attention and help. Being the sole support for another person, especially when that person has many significant or urgent needs, can be exhausting.

If you find yourself tiring out or becoming frustrated by the needs or demands of a survivor, please make sure to draw in additional help. It is far better to help the survivor learn to trust a larger set of competent people than to be her sole protector. Any person with only one trusted person in the world is in danger. It can feel good to be the most trusted person in another person's life, but after a while it can also be exhausting. Try to expand the survivor's circle of friends before you become exhausted. Don't wait until you already feel burdened and resentful.

2. Keep Your Own Emotional Balance.

Emotionally, we may be surprised by our limits. It is not unusual to hear someone else's story and to feel affected by it. Especially stories of bad things happening to children, extraordinarily severe situations of abuse, sexual torture or mutilation can be particularly emotionally affecting for many people. The content of a story can come close to our own lives in ways that wake up our own fears. On the other hand, sometimes it is not content but rather the way that we feel about the suffering person that makes it painful for us to hear her story.

A good rule is to notice your own reaction to someone else's pain. If you feel very affected or have a very strong reaction, positive or negative, pay attention. Extra strong urges to help, as well as strong feelings of disgust, anger, fear or confusion are clues for you. Make sure that if you are having a particularly strong reaction you talk about that reaction with your own friends and support people.

Strong emotions are a sign that we are being affected and may need to pay more attention to our own limits. It is not a bad thing to care about someone, but sometimes we can care in a way that is emotionally off balance. Notice strong reactions and make sure you keep your balance and remember your limits. If you are working professionally with survivors, this is a sign to talk with your supervisor.

For instance, we may be so upset by what has happened to one of our own children that we cannot think logically about what they need. We may try to help in ways that are more related to what we want than to what the child really needs. A mother may be very upset by what happened to her daughter and try to protect her from other people's judgments. She may tell her daughter not to talk about the abuse because she is afraid of the way the daughter could be hurt by other people's judgments. It may also be painful for the mother to hear the details of the abuse. But there are times when that silence may only increase her daughter's sense of helplessness and powerlessness.

On the other hand, a psychologist who is working with a survivor and has a very strong reaction to her experience may give inappropriate advice. For instance, for ideological reasons some therapists may push survivors to confront or to forgive their abusers before they are ready. Confrontation of abusers, or forgiveness of them is something that must be chosen by the survivor and must fit her recovery process. Other people should not choose the timing of these steps in a woman's recovery. Indeed, there are some survivors who never confront and some who never forgive their abusers.

When therapists or helpers try to push a survivor toward confrontation or forgiveness, the helper may actually be trying to help herself. The helper wants to feel comfortable with the outcome. The helper may believe that all abusers should have to face the consequences of their actions and be punished. Alternatively, the helper may feel that the best way for a survivor to heal is to forgive and make peace with the abuser. This choice must belong to the survivor, not to her helpers.

These are significant steps and choices in the healing process. These tasks certainly are not part of the early stages of recovery from abuse. Confronting an abuser or forgiving them is not an ideological choice; it must come from a place of psychological readiness, if it ever happens at all. If a helper becomes strongly attached to the way that she believes a survivor is supposed to recover, if the emotions a helper feels about the outcome are intense, the helper may have lost her own emotional balance.

3. Don't Let Someone Else's Crisis Become Yours

Helping without catching the feeling of crisis and urgency that a survivor feels is important. It is also very important that helpers not become too attached to a particular outcome for the recovery of a survivor. This way of keeping our boundaries is about remembering that the problem *and* the solution belong to the survivor herself.

A key part of healing from abuse is for the survivor to rebuild a sense of control over some aspects of her life after the helplessness and hopelessness invoked by trauma. Rediscovering her ability to identify and understand her own needs and desires is very important. When she understands her needs and desires, a survivor can act upon them. This is necessary if a person is going to move beyond being a victim into becoming a survivor. When helpers become controlling, they are no longer empowering.

It is not easy to remain calm and non-controlling about the final outcome when someone faces danger, great fear, or the risk of serious harm. Staying calm and keeping your own emotional balance when someone you care about is in real crisis requires discipline and awareness. But a calm mind and logical problem solving are things that a person in crisis cannot manage for herself. Her fear is real, her hurt is genuine, but she is often not able to make well reasoned decisions about safety and priorities. It is the job of a less frightened helper to help provide logical, balanced thinking.

It can be very tempting to take over, especially if we don't trust that our friend will be safe. But in the end our friend will have to take the main role in caring for herself, so she must be involved in choosing the solutions to her own crisis. This balance is often difficult to hold, but it may be one of the most important parts of being a trustworthy friend during a crisis.

4. Pay Close Attention To Your Own Needs When Helping Others.

Because our calm, cool, logical thinking is so important to helping effectively, very good self care is absolutely essential for helpers. We mentioned this before in the section on secondary trauma affecting the helper. It is worth mentioning this point again. The best care provider is someone who's own basic needs are met.

If I want to be good to other people, I need to be good to myself and have energy in reserve for the task. Because helping feels good, some helpers get lots of satisfaction just from being helpful. This is fine; satisfaction from doing good things is not a problem. However, the balance is off when we believe that the needs of others are so urgent that our own needs are no longer relevant.

There are some people who have the habit of taking care of everyone else but forgetting themselves. Selflessness can be admirable at times, but it often becomes a pathway to frustration, exhaustion and resentment. If you have begun to feel burdened by the helping work you do, if you feel angry or resentful that the demands of others are draining your energy, you are forgetting your own needs. When a helper, a true friend, helps him or herself too, it is like recharging a battery. The better the balance of care for ourselves along with care for others, the longer and the stronger our caring work can continue. We do not need to sacrifice ourselves, or become a martyr in the cause of helping. In fact, the most empowering help is help that strengthens everyone together. When you take good care of yourself, you provide a good example for the people you help.

If you are not sure how to take good care of yourself, please figure that out. Think about how you can regain your balance, feel refreshed and live in a way that is a good example for your friends. The best results strengthen everyone.

TRY THIS

Keeping Healthy Boundaries: Saying "No"

1. **Find a notebook and a pencil or pen** and set it beside you to take notes. Take a few deep breaths, make yourself comfortable, and focus your attention inside yourself.

2. **Think back and remember a time when you wanted to say no, but said yes.** Remember a time when a friend, a co-worker or a family member asked you to do something for them, to help them, and you didn't want to do it. Though you wanted to say no, you said yes.

3. **Notice your body sensations, your thoughts, your emotions.** How could you tell that you didn't want to help? What was the sign that you did not want to do this? Take note of those signs and remember them.

4. **Review in your mind what you did at the time.** How did you react to the body sensations, thoughts or emotions you felt then? What was

your reaction to the other person? Did the words, actions or feelings expressed by the other person affect the way you reacted? How? Just notice this.

5. Was there anything in particular about **your own body sensations,** thoughts or position that made you say yes when you wanted to say no? Notice this.

6. Was there anything in particular in **the other person's behavior,** in their words or actions that was especially hard for you to deal with? Please note specifically what the person said or did that "hooked" you and helped make you say yes when you wanted to say no.

7. **Focus on the thing that pushed you to say yes when you wanted to say no and just breathe with it for a few moments.** If it is a thought, notice that it is just a thought. If it is a sensation, notice that it is just a sensation. If it is something else, notice it and breathe into it. You don't have to change it, just notice it, label it for what it is in your mind. Notice if it stays the same or changes in any way.

8. **Ask yourself.** How important is this thought, feeling or sensation to me? Can I cope with it? Can I let it be there and say no anyway? What would be the likely consequences of acting on my urge to say yes? What would be the likely consequences of acting on my urge to say no?

9. **Take a few more breaths as you review this choice point.** Give yourself a few moments to breathe before imagining saying no. **Then say no calmly in your imagination.**

10. **Watch or feel what happens when you say no.** Go back to the body sensations, thoughts or emotions that were the signs you wanted to say no. Review them again, what has happened to them now?

11. **Rehearse the scene of saying no in your imagination** and notice any thoughts feelings or sensations that come up. Don't fight these reactions, accept them and just be aware of them.

142

12. Did anything about your experience seem different to you after doing this review? If not, maybe you are satisfied with saying yes to your friend, co-worker or family member. If anything changed and you feel differently now, review that again. Will this help you to say no in a similar situation next time? Why or why not?

4. Especially For Partners and Family Members of Sexual Abuse Survivors

a. Sexuality Issues

The family and especially husbands, boyfriends, and intimate partners of abuse survivors may recognize some special challenges in trying to support and help a survivor of sexual abuse recover. Because sexual abuse involves both sex and intimacy, there are significant affects on those areas of a survivor's life. As we mentioned in the first section on relationship effects for survivors after sexual abuse, there are two main patterns of sexual effects.

After abuse some survivors seem to have increased sexual urges or more desire to engage in sexual behaviors, even when those behaviors are risky or unsafe for them. This pattern is sometimes called becoming hyper-sexual. The other common pattern is a strong urge to avoid sex and sexuality. Often survivors also experience complications in their lives in the area of intimacy, or the ability to create healthy closeness with others and then maintain that closeness. Let's look briefly at each of these issues.

Hyper-sexuality may be an expression of different things. Some survivors say that they feel immoral and dirty anyway, so they might as well engage in risky sexual behaviors. If a woman imagines she is not honorable and desirable as a good woman, she may imagine that she can only be attractive to bad men. If she has already lost her honor, she may think she no longer has a reason to protect herself.

Alternatively, if she has come to associate attention from others mostly with sex, she may believe that in order to have attention from other people, she needs to be sexual with them. Perhaps abuse has made her think that she can only please people or hope for their love if she has sex with them. She may also feel desperate for attention and caring and may imagine that in order to be appealing, she has to be sexual. There are many different ways that survivors describe their reasons for seeking out lots of sex.

Some sexual abuse survivors say that they find themselves having sex with men they don't care about and then pushing them away as a way to hurt or punish them. Some survivors are angry about feeling used and use others for revenge in return. Usually this revenge feels empty and can become hurtful to the survivor too, but she may feel compelled. In fact, there are some people who find themselves behaving in ways that are compulsive or feel automatic and forced from within.

A drive to do things that may be hurtful to the self and that do not give satisfaction or increase well-being but lead to more risk instead, is a sign that sexual behavior is not healthy. If a survivor is behaving in these ways, she needs professional psychological help.

Another major pattern after sexual abuse is a strong desire to avoid sexuality and sexual behaviors altogether. Sex may seem frightening or dangerous when it has become associated with force and harm. A survivor may even love and care for a partner but not be able to relax, be receptive, and feel pleasure. Some common sexual problems are: lack of sexual desire, difficulty becoming aroused, and difficulty having orgasm. Even vaginismus, a painful tightening of the muscles around the opening of the vagina so that sexual intercourse is painful or impossible, may at times be associated with abuse.

Some women who are abused early in life may become so frightened by sex that they avoid relationships and closeness with men altogether. Some are afraid that they are defective, dirty or shameful and no decent man would be interested in them anyway. To avoid shame, they avoid closeness.

b. Trust and Intimacy

With or without these affects on sexual behavior there are often affects after abuse on intimacy or trusting close relationships. Closeness and trust can be difficult to rely upon after we have been violated by sexual abuse. Closeness is risky anyway, and can begin to seem too dangerous after we have been abused. Trust is built on the experience of success after taking risks. We learn to trust from interpersonal risk taking that has positive results.

When trust has had very negative results, we can lose our emotional balance and lose faith in trusting. Many survivors of abuse demonstrate contradictory behaviors. At the same time, they may have an intense desire to find trustworthy relationships and also a great deal of difficulty actually building and maintaining that trust.

Survivors may be too quick to trust people when there is little evidence of trustworthiness. They may also become unreasonably disappointed or hurt by people after relatively minor disappointments. We discussed this type of hyper-sensitivity and difficulty maintaining emotional balance in the first section of this guide on the effects of abuse. Especially when abuse begins in childhood, a survivor may not have developed good skills for understanding, testing and building trust.

Trust and learning to trust is one of the first, earliest tasks of psychological development. Ordinarily trust is something we first learn when we are babies and dependent upon our family and the people who care for us. If we have had major problems during that phase of our lives, or if we have had major disruptions later in relationships that we believed we could trust, the psychological consequences may be lasting. A survivor or her family and intimates may be able to identify a pattern in her life of disrupted trust or unbalanced efforts to make trusting connections and difficulty maintaining trust. Great sensitivity may lead to frequent disappointment. If a survivor is having serious problems making and keeping good relationships, if trust and closeness seem to be very problematic, she may benefit from seeking out skilled psychological help.

c. Strength after Healing, Real Intimacy

Many of us forget that building real intimacy is not easy, not a simple process. Real intimacy, genuine closeness, can be tested by disappointment and difficulties but still endures. People who have strong relationships are able to communicate and repair problems that come up between them. It is not that they do not ever have problems. After experiencing the extreme disappointment and violation of abuse, it is possible to become so sensitive and fearful that repair seems impossible. One of the reasons that a full recovery process is so important is because through recovery we can reestablish faith in the possibility of healing and repair. Survivors say over and over again in treatment that one of the most important things recovery does is help them to regain a feeling of hope.

Hope, trust and faith that even if differences and problems arise in relationships they can be overcome, is the foundation of intimacy. When we believe that problems in a relationship can be solved, we are able to take the risk of being authentic and close. Before recovering from abuse, survivors may have lost that faith. The strength they gain from recovery restores that faith. In the end some of the strongest relationships are relationships that have been tested but then deepened through authentic encounter, risk and repair. Without saying that abuse is beneficial, which it is not, we can say that sometimes people who have been tested and struggled with the difficulties of abuse are even stronger and have more depth than those who never had to overcome such big challenges.

Relationships with people who are able to risk authentic, deep connections can be especially satisfying. Significant strength and confidence can be gained from healing major losses and hurt. People who work with survivors of trauma and abuse sometimes describe "post traumatic growth" and "resilience" in their research. While we must never say that abuse is a good thing, it is not a reason for despair. The people who want to help trauma survivors may find that the relationships they can build with them, after patience, effort and even the struggle of recovery, can lead to great satisfaction.

Acting as a helper or partner or a true friend of a survivor of sexual abuse is often very challenging. This guide does not want to make light of the difficulties that true friends encounter. However, the benefits of learning to have and hold good boundaries, of finding our own emotional balance and learning to take good care of ourselves even as we care for others, are very great.

Becoming a true friend to a survivor of abuse or becoming a skilled helper in this area of work is a powerful way to develop and grow as a human being. If a helper engages in the process with awareness and skill, they gain strength and depth along with the people they help. Healing work then is an opportunity for mutual healing for everyone involved. The challenges may be great, but the rewards are also many.

5. What Services Does a Survivor Need?

Protect, Prosecute and Prevent

Because sexual abuse can affect so many different areas of life, it is important to be systematic and careful about identifying a survivor's needs and finding the right services for her. Each person's life and needs are unique, so there is no single plan for serving survivors that will fit everyone. However, a systematic step-by-step approach to assessing needs and then addressing them is most likely to be successful.

This guide will not describe all the many options that are available, nor all the services that a survivor and her family may need. A comprehensive discussion of services for adult abuse survivors is beyond the scope of this guide. Instead, we will briefly outline the types of services that an adult survivor might need and how to approach identifying and making a recovery plan with her.

Once again we must emphasize that for true recovery, a survivor must be able to identify her own needs and priorities and make her own choices. Help is important, but when others try to take over and decide what is best for a survivor instead of letting her make choices, she cannot recover fully.

We will use the metaphor that each survivor is taking a journey down a road to recovery after she encounters abuse. Here is a map to help direct her journey.

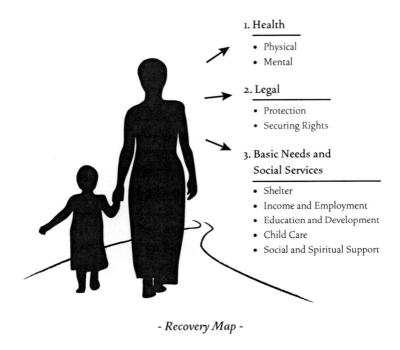

- Recovery Map -

The motto **Protect, Prosecute and Prevent** can be a useful guide for thinking about the goals of our Recovery Map journey. One of the first questions we must ask when we encounter a survivor is how recent was the last incident of abuse? If the abuse was a rape that has just occurred, we must immediately focus on the survivor's **medical health needs** and make sure that those needs are addressed in a way that also helps her to protect her legal rights.

To make sure a victim of rape becomes a survivor, a qualified medical professional must attend to any bodily injuries she may have and gather any evidence that may be necessary to pursue her legal right to protection. Evidence for legal proceedings must be gathered immediately and some of a woman's medical needs may be serious or urgent.

Though this can be very unpleasant for a survivor of recent abuse, she needs a medical examination and treatment immediately, even before washing, changing her clothing and cleaning herself up. For survivors of forcible sex acts, the urge to clean themselves is usually intense, so medical attention and gathering of evidence should not be delayed. Medical needs also can often become worse if treatment is postponed. Act quickly on medical needs.

Mental health needs can be complex and usually change over time. One way to think about psychological support is that in the immediate aftermath of abuse, and at the time that a survivor decides to take the enormous risk of talking about her abuse experience, the best approach for a helper is simply to listen and accept whatever she has to say. Judgments and questioning of her motives or questioning about the causes of the assault are generally not helpful. Pushing for additional information beyond what is necessary to protect her at this point is likely to be harmful. The question of blame is not the first priority, protection is.

Physical protection is a top priority; get the information necessary to make sure she is safe. For legal purposes, skilled people should gather the details of her story. They need training to gather relevant information without causing a survivor additional psychological harm. This is a task for legal professionals.

After a survivor has been listened to without judgment, when her basic needs for security and protection have been addressed, then she may be ready to give more details of her abuse story. First a helper must demonstrate that they can be trusted to be kind and competent with painful information. This is part of psychological protection. Do not be surprised if a woman gives new details and adds new information to her story as she becomes more comfortable and feels safer with her interviewers. This is normal and indicates that she is beginning to recover from the worst of her fear.

This does not indicate she has not been telling the truth. Survivors regularly leave information out and cover up parts of their stories to protect themselves, as we have discussed in other parts of this book.

There are **legal issues** related to protection, for instance whether she needs a legal protection order against the abuser, or whether she or her children are still at risk from the abuser if he is a family member. These legal needs should be addressed first, to ensure her safety. Next you may consider other legal needs she may have that secure her rights.

Her needs may vary depending on her relationship to the abuser, further risks to her life or to her longer term well being. Some survivors consider divorce from an abusive spouse, some pursue other ways of protecting themselves or their children legally. When an abuser is a family member it can be very delicate deciding how to protect her. But no matter whom the abuser is, the victim of a crime like sexual abuse deserves protection and the abuser must be held accountable for the crime. It is very important that a woman talks to and gets good advice from someone trained and knowledgeable about women's legal rights and interpersonal violence.

Once her immediate and urgent health, safety and legal issues have been addressed, many survivors have additional needs for social services. Again these needs will vary from survivor to survivor but everyone needs to have a secure, safe place to live, and enough food, clothing and medical care to stay healthy. Then as time goes on, opportunities for employment, education and economic support are important to survivors' personal empowerment.

When abuse happens within families, it can be especially complicated to serve all of a survivor's basic needs; the needs of one individual do not always correspond easily with the needs of a whole family. But a victim of sexual violence should not be sacrificed for the benefit of her family. In the end, the whole family and everyone around the family will suffer if the rights and needs of individuals are not served. Balancing individual and family needs should not happen at the long term expense of either the survivor or the well-being of other vulnerable family members like children.

Many people who are survivors of multiple incidents or types of abuse have begun to live in a very narrow and restricted world. They may not know what it is like to have their basic needs for food, shelter and health met. But beyond that, they may also have lived without the benefit of enough education, their social lives may have become restricted and they may not feel able to live a full, satisfying life. Even survivors who have lived in comfortable social and economic circumstances sometimes experience a narrowing of their mental horizons because of the psychological effects of abuse. Many survivors of complicated or longer term abuse live psychologically restricted lives and feel unrealistically helpless or hopeless.

Opportunities for pleasure, joy, exercising the imagination, having fun, and spiritual support are important to every person, survivors included. First meeting basic needs and then considering goals for personal empowerment is the role of social service workers, friends and social advocates for survivors. This is at the core of preventing future abuse for individual survivors.

Employment may open up a survivor's world or keep her in a trap of underachievement. Empowerment includes education and psychological support to imagine achievable and appealing life goals. Many survivors have not considered what they really want for themselves and what kinds of education, work or social activity would be satisfying for them. A full recovery with good social support will explore these questions. Social service workers, friends and caring family members can help a survivor to think about her own dreams, goals and preferences so that she pursues a journey toward a life she can truly call her own, a life she has chosen.

Interviewing Survivors

Steps to Remember:

When you are in a professional or voluntary helping role serving survivors of sexual abuse, in addition to thinking about what kinds of needs she may have, skilled helpers will pay attention to:

1. **The helper's role:** If you are a helping professional or volunteer, begin your interview by giving a survivor this information about your role. What is the helper's role in this survivor's life and what type of help is she or he in a position to offer? Helpers should be clear about this role first in their own minds and make sure that the survivor understands this role too.

2. **The helper's goals:** As part of explaining your role, it is good to identify the goals you have for assisting the survivor. Make sure you are clear about your own goals and that you have communicated them accurately to her.

3. **The survivor's goals:** What does she hope for as an outcome from the help you can offer? Once you have outlined your role and goals, ask her about her goals. Does she have a realistic idea of what you are offering? Is there a match between your goals and hers? If there is not a match, can you still help her with her goals? If you do not want to or cannot help her to reach the goals she has identified, is there anyone else who can? Can you refer her?

4. **Listen non-judgmentally:** There are times when the most valuable thing we can offer to a survivor is non-judgmental listening. This is not a small thing to offer. This is a very precious gift if you are genuine, respectful and willing. Sometimes we expect too much of ourselves or of the survivor. Never underestimate the value of a good non-judgmental listener and empathy.

5. **Clarify your limits:** If you know your limits and communicate them clearly, you are protecting yourself and the survivor. If a survivor is asking you to do things that you cannot do, or that you do not have the knowledge

and skill to offer, make that clear. Don't try to stretch past your limits; this can be harmful to both of you.

6. **Have a plan:** A true friend and skilled helper can think rationally and make logical plans to attain goals when the survivor does not have the presence of mind to do so. Because survivors are talking about very emotional, complicated topics, it is often very difficult for them to be rational and make good logical plans to reach their goals.

7. **Follow up:** When you make a plan to help a survivor, be sure to keep track of the responsibilities that you have taken and in addition follow up on the responsibilities that the survivor has taken. Often survivors have difficulties keeping track of goals, plans and tasks, either because of limited knowledge or because of complicated and disorganized life situations. A skilled helper can keep track and follow up.

8. **Self care:** Don't forget to take good care of yourself. Notice when you are feeling any mental or emotional effects from working with survivors. Have a good routine for rest, relaxation and rejuvenation.

The following pair of exercises may be helpful to people who have been helping survivors of trauma. The first exercise helps us to become more aware of sensations in our bodies that we may or may not be paying attention to in our daily life. Noticing what we feel, being aware or mindful of our bodies, can help us to notice when the helping that we do is taking a toll on us.

TRY THIS

Body Scan[03]

- Find a quiet place where you will not be interrupted for about 10 minutes and make yourself physically comfortable. Some people like to sit in a chair; some people prefer to lie flat on their back with their feet on the floor and knees bent.
- Close your eyes or let your focus go soft. Most people find it easiest to pay attention to internal sensations when they do not focus or look at things outside and around them.
- Focus your internal attention on the soles of your feet. Take a couple of full body breaths like those in the earlier exercises. Imagine that your breath is passing through the soles of your feet into the floor. Imagine that your breath comes in through your nose, travels all the way down through your trunk, then through your legs until it reaches your feet. Breathe out as if through the soles of your feet. In this way imagine yourself taking full breaths and breathing through your feet.
- As you take these breaths through the soles of your feet notice any sensations there. You may notice the contact that your feet have with the floor or with the insides of your shoes. You may notice tension or looseness, you may feel pain or relaxation, you may feel nothing there at all. Whatever you notice, just note it in your mind and continue to breathe. You don't need to change anything, just pay attention.
- Now let your attention move up to your ankles. Focus your attention on your ankles and let your full breath move through your ankles. Imagine that your ankles are the place where you breathe, and breathe in and out noticing any sensations that you notice there. Are they cold or hot?

---

[03] This exercise is based on one developed by Jon Kabat-Zinn in *Full Catastrophe Living*

Do you feel tightness or looseness, hardness or softness? Do you feel nothing there at all? Whatever you feel, just notice it and breathe.

- **Now let your attention move up to your lower legs.** Breathe in and out through your lower legs, your calves and shins. Pay attention to any sensations you find there. Are they hard or soft? Relaxed or tense? Just notice and breathe; you don't need to change anything.
- **Now let your attention move up into your knees and thighs.** Breathe in and out through your knees and upper legs. Notice anything at all that you feel in your upper legs. Are they warm? Can you feel them all the way from your knees to your pelvis? Just notice and breathe.
- **Bring your attention up into your pelvis.** Breath through your pelvis and note any sensations, or lack of sensation that you find here. Sometimes the main thing we notice about a body part is that we don't have sensations there. Sometimes our attention to a body part brings other thoughts or emotions to awareness. If anything like that happens, just notice it and continue to breathe through it. Let the thoughts, feelings and sensations come up and continue to breathe. You do not need to do anything about any of this. Just let it come and then let it go.
- **Now let your attention move up into your lower belly.** Again, pay attention to any sensations you have in your lower belly as you breathe through it. Feel yourself breathing in and out through your lower belly, nice full breaths. Is it relaxed or tight? Warm or cold? Do you have any sensations there at all? Just notice them and breathe.
- **Bring your attention up into your belly.** Breath through your solar plexus, or diaphragm and notice. Is it soft or hard? Do you have any discomfort or is your belly comfortable? Does it rise and fall easily with your breath? Just notice whatever you notice as you breathe through your belly.
- **Now bring your attention up into your chest.** Feel your chest expand and contract as you breathe through your chest. If you notice any sen-

sations there just breathe into them and let them be. No need to change anything, we are just noticing. Tension, looseness, relaxation or tightness, just take note of it and continue to breathe.

- **Bring your attention up into your shoulders and neck.** Many people carry tension or stress in their neck and shoulders. If you do that, just notice it and continue to breathe. Let each breath move through your neck and shoulders and notice any sensations you may hold there. You don't have to change what you feel, but notice it and breathe.
- **Let your attention move to your arms.** Breathe through your arms and notice any sensations that you may find there. In your upper arms, elbows, forearms, wrists, hands, and fingers. Breathe through your arms a few moments.
- **Now pay attention to your face and jaw.** Feel the muscles around your lips and eyes, your cheeks and tongue. Breathe through your face noticing any sensations- tightness, warmth, looseness, tiredness, tingling. Whatever you feel in your face, just notice it and breathe through it.
- **Finally, let your attention move up to the top of your head and your whole scalp.** Notice anything at all that you feel in your scalp and head. Can you feel your hair? Breathe.
- **Now imagine that a hole, like the blowhole of a whale or a dolphin has opened in the top of your head.** Let your breath come and go freely through that blowhole in the top of your head. Let the breath come in through the top of your head and then go all the way down through your head, neck, chest, belly, legs and feet - then out through your toes. Feel the breath as if it is moving through your entire body. As if you are breathing through your entire body from the top of your head down to the tips of your toes. Feel the rocking sensation as you take a few of these full and complete body breaths.

- **Notice anything you notice in your body as you take these full body breaths.** Take a moment to sweep your attention through your whole body, from your toes to your legs, to your torso, through your arms, to your head. Do you notice anything new? Is everything just the same as it was? Take note of whatever you find. Continue to breathe. Complete the scan of your whole body and just notice.
- **When you have completed this scan, let your attention come back to the room.** Open your eyes or refocus your attention gently on the room where you have been doing the exercise. Take your time as you go back to your normal activities and remember anything you learned from the body scan that may be helpful to you.

The final exercise we want to offer is a guided imagery that may help you to rest, relax and rejuvenate yourself. This is designed to offer a mini vacation that you can give to yourself whenever you choose. These images may be helpful to you. However, if these specific images are not restful for you, then feel free to create a visual imagery exercise that you find more restful and rejuvenating. Everyone is different, but everyone also has a need to recharge his or her batteries. You can do this along with the body scan or all by itself. You can do this alone or in a group.

TRY THIS

Rest, Relax and Rejuvenate: Guided Imagery[04]

- **Make yourself comfortable.** Some people like to sit, some like to lie down. You may choose to darken the room or close your eyes. Make yourself as comfortable as you can, and breathe. Take a couple of full,

---

[04] Based on an exercise by Christine Payne-Towler.

deep breaths, in through your nose and out through your mouth. Signal to your body that it can let go.

- **As you breathe, let your breath carry away any tension you may have been holding.** With each breath, feel yourself bathed in a stream of gentle, warm water. The water is washing over you and carrying away any tension and stress that you may have held.
- **Let the water carry away any thoughts, sensations, tensions or stress that you don't need.** The water is warm enough to be comfortable, cool enough to be refreshing. It carries away everything that is unnecessary, everything uncomfortable. It washes things away in a flow, taking what you don't need and moving it along down stream, out of your life, far far away.
- **Just let yourself feel the stream wash over and cleanse you for a few breaths.**
- **Now notice that you feel a gentle breeze.** The stream of water is gone. A breeze is blowing softly on your face and ruffling your hair. It is a warm and refreshing breeze. Just strong enough to dry you off after the stream of water, but not strong enough to make you uncomfortable. The breeze is fresh and gentle. Feel it blow around you. It brings pleasant scents and sounds. It dries you softly and refreshes you so you feel clean and energized.
- **As you continue to breathe, let your attention drop down to your contact with the floor or the chair. Let your attention drop to the base of your spine.** Now notice that out of the base of your spine, you are sprouting roots. Roots are dropping down from the base of your spine into the earth below you. The roots drop down through the floor, through whatever is below you, seeking the earth below you. Let them go down.
- **As your roots drop down through the earth, notice that you are becoming like a tree.** Your roots are seeking the darkness and holding firm

in the soil that is below you. As your roots drop down, you feel them in the earth, pushing down through rocks and soil, around any barriers they find. Your roots are strong and flexible.

- **Now notice your trunk.** As your roots hold you firmly on the earth, notice the trunk of your tree. What kind of a tree have you become? Do you have leaves or needles? Do your branches spread wide or reach straight up? Do you bear fruit or flowers? Just notice what kind of a tree you are. Notice anything you can about this tree and the things around it. While you are imagining this, don't forget to breathe.
- **When you are sure of your tree** and can feel the roots that ground you and the trunk that holds you up, notice that energy from the earth comes up through your roots and out through your branches, twigs and leaves. Notice the way that your tree can pull up energy from the ground and grow. Notice the way that your leaves or needles take in the energy of sunlight and make it into living food for the tree. The sunlight feeds you. The earth holds you strong. Breathe and feel your strength and energy from your roots through your branches twigs and leaves breathing as a tree.
- **Finally, let yourself come back to the room.** When you have taken some time to breathe and drink in the energy from your tree, let yourself return. Bring back the energy, the strength and the vitality you felt when you were bathed in the water, soothed by the breeze and stood strong as the tree. Carry these sensations with you as you go back to your ordinary day.

6. Strength After Healing Together

A Systemic Approach

Sexual abuse, violence in families, and the severe and lasting effects that can result from them are ugly and distressing topics. Talking about these kinds of interactions and the way that people are damaged by them is not something that anyone enjoys. Most of us would rather turn away, think about other things and hope that somehow these problems will simply go away. But it is clear that these issues have been with us and unresolved for thousands of years of human history. Turning away, covering them up, or wishing them gone will not solve these problems; humanity has tried those methods for a very long time indeed.

Of course there are also those who would say that these problems are simply unsolvable. There is an argument that these bad behaviors are just a part of human nature, there are some bad people who will always be abusive and the best we can do is punish or eliminate these evil people. Many people see victims as the unfortunate people who fall prey to bad people, or who somehow bring harm upon themselves. No one thinks sexual abuse and family violence are good things. Some people just believe it probably cannot be solved. This view is deeply pessimistic and has also been around for a very long time.

This guide is written from quite a different point of view. Instead of looking at sexual abuse and violence in families as sad, sick phenomena isolated to a few bad, unfortunate people or unhappy families. Instead of seeing abuse as a sign of moral weakness, we take a different view. Widespread phenomena like sexual abuse and family violence are not moral problems in otherwise good societies; they are signs that there are problems built into the structures and systems of the societies where they are common. Sexual abuse and family violence reflect basic confusion among people in much of the world about how social, biological, living systems work.

While we may never eliminate sexual and family violence altogether, it is clear that in some places and in some systems, people have been able to reduce them significantly. While no one method has been shown scientifically to be effective in all places, there is evidence that we can reduce sexual abuse most effectively through systematic prevention. If prevention and reduction of sexual abuse and family violence is our real goal, we need to understand what we describe as taking a systemic approach. Let's look more closely at what we mean by a systemic approach and how taking such an approach can benefit everyone in a society.

An Ant's World System

In order to understand a systemic point of view it may be helpful to use another metaphor. Let's imagine that we are looking at the world from the point of view of an ant.

An ant is a social creature that lives in colonies. Considering the ant itself, we have an individual animal with a separate existence. In turn, the ant is made up of a system of organs and biological parts that work together to keep it alive. Those organs, tissues, and cells can in turn be broken down into their component parts of molecular, chemical structures, which can then be broken down even further into elements and atomic structures. In short, an individual ant is made up of a complex set of biological structures made up of component parts that nest within each other and function together to make up the living organism that is the ant.

If we look at the ant's world system in the other direction, we find that ants live in colonies or groups of ants that live together in a way that keeps individual ants alive. One ant alone will die if it is separated for long from

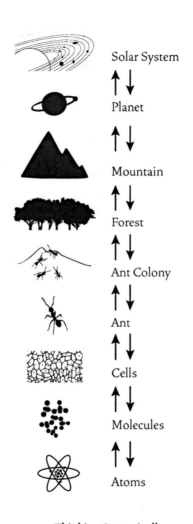

*- Thinking Systemically,
An Ant's World of Nested Realities -*

its colony. The ant colony in turn is part of a broader ecosystem, for instance a forest, and that forest ecosystem is in turn part of a wider living ecosystem, say a mountain, which is part of a mountain range, which is part of a continent, on up to the whole planet, on up to the solar system and so on.

Each part of the ant's world system is part of a wider whole and each whole then is part of a yet wider whole, "all the way up and all the way down". A philosopher named Ken Wilber uses metaphors like this one to illustrate the way that the whole world and everything in it is at one and the same time both a part and a whole. Every living thing, like the ant, is a part and also a whole. There are no exceptions to this rule; people and social systems are included.

So what does it mean to be at the same time both a part and a whole, and what difference does this make to our topic of sexual abuse and family violence? According to this metaphor, problems in systems occur when any part of the system forgets that it is at one and the same time both a part and a whole. Each part of the system is essential to its existence. Every part is necessary to make up the whole. Wholes, at the same time, must never lose track of the necessity to be a part of yet another whole further up the nested system of realities.

A part may become too fond of its own "wholeness" and begin to promote itself at the expense of any of the parts making it up. Any whole that loses track of the vital importance of each and every part within it and ceases to try to keep that inner system of parts functioning together in a dynamic, balanced way will fall apart. Any of these wholes or parts that forget their place in the system and unbalance the system's functioning by trying to dominate and promote their own existence at the expense of other parts or wholes, are actually damaging the whole system including themselves.

Eventually, when the damage caused by this kind of dominance becomes great enough, the whole system is at risk for breaking down. If an ant forgets it is part of the colony and tries to leave, it will die.

On the other hand, if it tries to take over the colony and promote its own individual needs to the exclusion of the needs of the other ants, eventually the whole colony, including the domineering ant, will die.

When a part tries to act as a whole, forgetting that it depends upon its parts, for a time, sometimes for a long time, all the parts will try to reorganize themselves to maintain and preserve the existence of the whole system. Let's take the example of a family for instance.

There are times when a father and husband may forget to pay attention to the needs and value of all the members of his family. If he begins to imagine that the family exists simply to serve his needs, if he considers the needs of any other family members unimportant, eventually the family will break down. As family members are hurt or damaged by having their needs for health, well being and development neglected or even violated, they become weaker. As the parts of the family system become weaker under this kind of unbalanced domination, the whole family becomes weaker.

A family system will struggle in whatever ways it can to keep going and protect its existence when under this threat. The weakened parts will distort their functioning to try to balance the system, but eventually badly unbalanced systems with weakened parts cannot be sustained. When the family that was the father or husband's system for support falls apart, he too loses his position, his strength and he may even eventually lose his life. This is the danger of trying to become a dominant whole at the expense of one's own parts.

Sexual abuse, exploitation, neglect and family violence are all examples of this kind of dangerous, distorted, out-of-balance domination within a system. Whether these damaging violations of power occur within families or in the wider society outside families, they reflect the same problem. No part should ever forget that it is a part of a larger whole and that its individual existence depends upon a complex set of relationships of balanced needs and responsibilities.

When any part forgets its position in the wider systemic whole, it begins to damage the whole, including itself. Abusive people harm not only their victims but also themselves. Social systems that do not act to protect the people within them, that do not hold all of their members responsible for balanced behavior within the system, and do not prevent the imbalances and distortions that lead to abusive, exploitative and damaging interactions, will eventually break down.

So we are all part of the social whole that holds families and societies, nations and humanity. Because we are all parts of this whole, then we all depend upon its health and well being. I have a stake in the health of every other person who is a part of humanity. If other parts of the human whole are suffering with abuse, exploitation, neglect or violence, I too am being damaged as a part of that whole.

Women, men, adults, children, people of all nationalities, ethnicities, religious and cultural backgrounds, all of us have a vital stake in the well being of others, for better or worse. It's a pretty big responsibility. The good side is that others have just as big a stake in my well being as I have in theirs. We are working on this together, whether we are aware of that or not.

7. Balancing a Human Rights Orientation with a Social Contract

In some parts of the world issues of family violence and sexual abuse are most often viewed in terms of individual human rights. Women and children and exploited people have human rights and their rights need to be protected.

In some parts of the world more focus is placed on maintaining a strong fabric of social life and harmonious social relationships. In these more relational societies, there is a belief that we have a social contract and that the positions that we hold in relation to one another within a society are the key to assuring a good social life.

According to our ant's world metaphor both of these points of view are correct. The individual human rights orientation takes a human individual 'part' as its focus and wants to organize the system with that ant at its center. The social fabric orientation focuses first on a larger sense of the social 'whole' and the way that parts must be well organized and balanced within that whole. Attention to both the needs of the individual person as a part, and also to accountability to a social whole are necessary to keep systems balanced and healthy. Both points of view are correct and need to be held in balance.

Our work to protect every part, ensuring that the needs of each part are met, can be balanced with holding every part accountable to its position in the whole. We can keep both these levels of interest in mind with every step we take and at the same time promote understanding of this integrated point of view about both needs and accountability.

This balanced approach provides a foundation for prevention. Too much focus on individual rights or on simply maintaining the social order will hamper prevention. Unbalanced relational patterns lead to abuse, exploitation, neglect and violence. Based on cultural habits and value patterns, societies tend to lean toward one side or the other of this balance. But if we can learn from the strengths in all societies or cultures, if we can gain from the wisdom of a range of social systems and values, we can create systems that promote the well being of all people in all societies.

Working to solve the problem of sexual abuse and family violence gives us an opportunity to create a new way of working together to be a stronger human whole. As families grow healthier and stronger, and at the same time individuals grow healthier and stronger, the whole human system will thrive. Equal legal rights for individuals can be coupled with systems of social justice so that everyone is held accountable and expects to be responsible to the whole as well as to benefit as a part.

It is possible to think about healing sexual abuse and family violence as a part of a movement that aims toward healing the whole human system. The suffering we seek to heal is the inappropriate use of power and domination. Systems based primarily on domination and submission damage the whole human system.

We are not all the same. The goal of giving equal value to all parts is not the same as the goal of making everyone the same. Conformity of all parts to something dictated by a dominant force is not health. The dominant force, if there is one, should be our wholeness together.

Equality is not sameness. Women do not need to be just like men, children do not need to be just like adults, people from one society, religious or ethnic group do not need to be just like those from another. On the contrary, our differences are a very important part of what we contribute to the health of the whole social system. A complex system with different and strong component parts is the strongest system.

Differences are often not easy to deal with. In fact, if we are honest, we have to admit that differences between people are one of the hardest things we have to deal with in social life. Difference creates the potential for conflict. But without differences and without the skills to work through those differences, we cannot solve social problems. Differences help us to come up with creative solutions that keep our social systems functioning well.

Paradoxically, the things that challenge us, like social problems, and the fear and hurt of sexual abuse and violence, teach us what we need to know to become stronger. Societies with the courage and strength to face and work on healing these deep and painful challenges have the opportunity to become the strongest, most resilient and best socially developed societies in the world. This is a story and a world worth creating together.

GLOSSARY

Sexual Abuse- Sexual abuse in this guide is defined as any unwanted sexual behavior that is acted out upon another person by force, coercion or persuasion. Abuse or exploitation refers to the power difference between a dominant person who acts in an unwanted way on a person who is subordinate to them.

Emotional Balance- Emotional balance refers to the way that one manages the normal changes in emotional mood and energy that are a part of every person's life. As we have all experienced, there are skills that help us to cope in balanced and calmer ways. Traumatic experiences disturb this emotional balance.

Discipline- The capacity or the process of organizing and managing one's behavior so that one can reach goals or realize values.

Ideological Choice- A choice or value based upon an ideological position. This may involve choices for other people or for ourselves.

Abuser- A person who exploits his superior power or social position to meet his own needs without regard for the needs or wishes of others. This person dominates others at their expense for his own gain.

Survivor- A person who has experienced exploitation or abuse. With this term we emphasize that she has turned her attention toward recovery and is living her life after abuse with the aim of becoming whole again. The body-mind injuries a person may have sustained from the abuse can heal. Where we put our attention matters.

Non-Controlling Behavior- When a person is able to be with others without having to control or manage their behavior. A non-controlling person gives authority over others' lives to them and values others' perceptions of their own needs and wishes.

Rescuer- A person who aims to recue others from harm and does not believe victims have the capacity to do important things to help themselves. A person who helps others from a dominant position, instead of supporting the development of strength in the person who needs help.

Victim- A person who views themselves, or is viewed by others as a helpless or relatively powerless person, struggling to save themselves or protect themselves from harm.

Ultimate Result- The ultimate or final result of a process. The logical conclusion of a course of action.

Confidence- Strength and trust in one's self. A quality that is built upon a psychological and behavioral process of discovering and developing personal strengths and competencies.

Mental Health Professional- A person who is trained to understand and intervene effectively with mental health problems. This person may be a psychiatrist, a psychologist, a physician, a counselor, a nurse or any person with special training and supervision who understands the treatment of mental health disorders.

Risk- A situation in which there is the possibility of failure as well as success. A situation where the outcome may be good or bad.

Trauma- An experience that threatens or is perceived to threaten the health, well being, life or bodily integrity of a person, or of people with whom we feel close. There is usually an unexpected and always an overwhelming quality to traumatic experience.

Resources & References

Bass, Ellen & Davis, Laura 1988, **The Courage to Heal: A Guide for Women Survivors of Child Sexual Abuse.** New York: Harper and Row.

Dolan, Yvonne. 1991. **Resolving Sexual Abuse: Solution Focused Therapy and Ericksonian Hypnosis for Adult Survivors.** New York: W.W. Norton &Co.

Herman, Judith Lewis. 1992. **Trauma and Recovery.** New York: Basic Books.

Kabat-Zinn, Jon. 1990. **Full Catastrophe Living: Using the Wisdom of Your Body and Mind to Face Stress, Pain and Illness.** New York: Dell Publishing.

Karpman, Stephen. **The Karpman Drama Triangle.** Retrieved from *http://www. karpmandramatriangle.com/* 11-10-2011.

Nieto, Leticia. Boyer, Margot. 2010. **Beyond Inclusion, Beyond Empowerment: A Developmental Strategy to Liberate Everyone.** Olympia WA: Cuetzpalin Publishing.

Wilber, Ken 2000. **A Brief History of Everything.** Boston: Shambala.

Yoder, Carolyn, 2005. **The Little Book of Trauma Healing: When Violence Strikes and Community Security is Threatened.** Intercourse PA: Good Books.

TRUE FRIEND-
FOR WOMEN WHO HAVE EXPERIENCED SEXUAL ABUSE:
HOW TO BE A FRIEND TO YOURSELF
HOW TO BE A TRUE FRIEND TO A SURVIVOR

This book is a compact self help guide for women who have been sexually abused and for their relatives, friends and the people who provide services to them. In clear, accessible language the book describes the physiological, psychological and social effects of interpersonal trauma, offers practical exercises and activities that survivors can use to help calm and soothe themselves, and provides information and advice for people who want to be helpful to survivors. The book is appropriate for a wide audience and is especially designed for places where people may not have ready access to an established infrastructure of social and mental health services. It takes a positive, reassuring approach to trauma recovery, is based on cognitive behavioral and mindfulness treatment methods, and is particularly focused on the healing possibilities of healthy relationships. Published first in Turkish and distributed around Turkey in two separate editions, this book has been successfully used by all kinds of service professionals from police and lawyers to psychologists and counselors, as well as survivors themselves. This is a community oriented self help guide to a common, world wide social problem. Designed for international English speaking audiences and for translation *and* adaptation into other languages.

ABOUT THE AUTHOR

Leyla Welkin is a clinical cross cultural psychologist who has practiced psychotherapy, taught as an intercultural educator and developed programs in those fields for thirty years. Her birth in Gaziantep, Turkey to American parents began a life lived between many cultural worlds. She received her interdisciplinary Master's and Doctoral degrees in the United States and worked for many years there in outpatient clinics and in private practice with women and families struggling with the effects of sexual and family abuse. She also began teaching in university psychology and counseling programs in 1995. In 2008 Leyla returned to Turkey and founded the Pomegranate Connection program in Ankara. She continues to provide research, training and consultation services internationally and can be reached at welkin.l@gmx.com

CPSIA information can be obtained at www.ICGtesting.com
Printed in the USA
BVOW05s2230120514

352936BV00001B/2/P